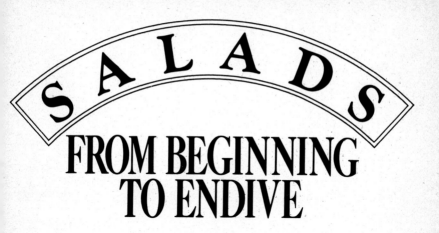

SALADS
FROM BEGINNING
TO ENDIVE

From KRAFT

D1567806

A Benjamin Company Book

Recipes and Editorial: The Kraft Kitchens

Photography: Kraft, Inc.
                      Creative Services

Copyright © 1980 Kraft, Inc.
ISBN 0-87502-073-9
Library of Congress Catalog Card Number 79-54947
All Rights Reserved
All trademarks are owned by Kraft, Inc.

Published by The Benjamin Company, Inc.
485 Madison Avenue
New York, N.Y. 10022

Printed in the United States of America
First Printing: February, 1980

Table of Contents

INTRODUCTION

Salads provide attractive colors, appealing flavors, interesting shapes, contrasting textures and important nutrients to a meal. They can be sweet or spicy, light or hearty. They can be the center of attention or a graceful accompaniment — whatever fits the menu and the occasion. No wonder salads are a favorite American food!

In this book you will find recipes to suit every need — portable fare for picnics, gourmet salads for entertaining, hearty main dish recipes, and snacks for the diet-conscious and many others. You'll also find helpful information about selecting salad ingredients, preparing and serving salads and for matching salads with appropriate dressings.

We hope these salad recipes will become regular family favorites.

History of Salads

Early salads consisted of grasses, herbs and other forms of vegetation served with salt as the dressing. Salads sprinkled with salt were especially enjoyed by the Romans. In fact, salt on greens was such a familiar combination that the Latin word for salt (sal) became the origin of the word "salad."

Salads were often served to clear the palate for the next course of a meal. Persians, for example, served salads with oil and vinegar or yogurt flavored with spices between the meat course and dessert.

According to Homer, the Greeks believed salads were a favored food of the gods. A typical meal for a Grecian gentleman was roasted or broiled meat, bread, cheese and dessert followed by a crisp fresh vegetable salad.

Centuries later, salads gained prestige in the courts of the European monarchs where royal chefs used such exotic ingredients as angelica, primrose and violets, elevating salad making to a culinary art. In eighteenth century France, salads were so fashionable that chefs frequently engaged in contests to create new delicacies for the nobles.

In the early years of this country, salads were enjoyed equally by people of all social levels. Favorite family recipes were shared with friends and neighbors and were adapted to include the fruits and vegetables native to America — corn, squash, a variety of beans and berries and many others. The popularity of salads is in evidence today in homes and restaurants across the nation.

History of Dressings

Salt was the first and only dressing for centuries until the Egyptians experimented with oil and vinegar. Several of today's familiar dressings, however, can be traced directly to France. The most famous pourable dressing is French dressing, which is traditionally a combination of oil and vinegar or lemon juice. Today there are many variations of the original. Americans are most familiar with the creamy red or orange versions.

Mayonnaise also made its debut in France at a banquet two hundred years ago when the Duc de Richelieu created the elegant dressing for his guests. He named it "Mahonaise" in honor of a French seaport where he had been victorious over the British in a naval battle. Mayonnaise was made commercially available in the United States in the 1920s and has continued to be a favorite.

A close relative of mayonnaise is "boiled" salad dressing which was equally popular but time-consuming to make at home. In the 1930s, American manufacturers made this kind of salad dressing available in a convenient form. The most popular brand today is Miracle Whip salad dressing.

There are two different stories about the origin of Thousand Island Dressing. One claims it was created by the chef of Chicago's Blackstone Hotel and named Blackstone Dressing, then renamed Thousand Island Dressing. The other story claims it originated in the Thousand Islands of the St. Lawrence River. Whatever its origin, Thousand Island is one of today's most popular dressings.

Few other countries have the broad selection of salad ingredients and dressings that the United States enjoys today. Convenient dressings in ready-to-serve form, a plentiful selection of produce and home refrigeration have been a great stimulus to the increasing popularity of salads. In most homes, salads are now a major part of at least one meal each day and are quite often served as the main course. Their great versatility and ease of preparation make them especially popular and a natural for today's casual entertaining.

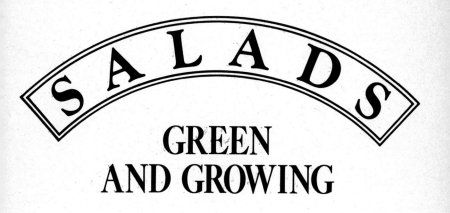

SALADS

GREEN AND GROWING

Endive, savoy cabbage, watercress and romaine may not be the most common salad greens; however, they offer great variety. Most are available at a nearby supermarket or from your own backyard garden.

With such a selection of greens in varying shades, shapes, textures and flavors, even a simple salad of assorted greens can be an imaginative creation. Picture a leafy combination of curly endive, velvety Boston lettuce and deep green spinach topped with crunchy croutons and seasoned with a savory dress-ing. This deceptively simple salad can be an attrac-tive, appetizing highlight for family meals or dinner parties.

Greens are also one of the most versatile salad in-gredients. They are the predominant ingredients in tossed salads and are excellent liners for salad bowls, plates or platters. Small, delicate greens such as watercress and parsley are decorative garnishes for almost any salad.

Salad greens are quite perishable; therefore, extra care is necessary to protect their color, flavor, texture and nutrient content. Follow these guidelines and fragile greens will stay crisp and flavorful for several days.

- At the supermarket, select greens that have crisp leaves and are relatively free of blemishes.
- After purchasing, immediately take greens home and prepare for storage.
- Wash gently under cool running water to remove sand or dirt. Drain quickly or pat dry with towels.
- Remove all brown spots and handle greens as lit-tle as possible.
- Store in plastic bags or in the crisper drawer of the refrigerator.
- Chill greens several hours before using so that they will be crisp and cold.

Although iceberg lettuce is the most popular, look for some of the more unusual salad greens in the fresh produce department. Explore and enjoy!

Lettuce is available in many varieties.

 Iceberg lettuce (or crisphead) grows in a compact round head with medium green outer leaves and pale green inner leaves. It has a crisp moist texture and a mild flavor.

 Leaf lettuce (or bunching lettuce) has long loose leaves growing from a center stem, but does not form a head. Medium to deep green in color, the leaves have a ruffled outer edge. Another variety, red leaf lettuce, is noted for its red-tipped leaves.

 Bibb, a type of butterhead lettuce, grows in a small head of loose, cupped leaves that are sweet and tender. It has dark green outer leaves and light green to yellow inner leaves.

 Boston, another type of butterhead lettuce, is medium to light green in color. The leaves have a velvety texture, separate easily from the head and have a delicate flavor.

Romaine (or Cos) is an elongated head of firm dark green to yellow leaves that are coarse in texture and slightly sharp to bitter in flavor.

Cabbage is available in four varieties.

 Green cabbage is pale green in color and forms a very tight round head of smooth, fine textured leaves. It has a pungent flavor.

 Red cabbage is similar to the green variety but has a reddish-purple color. It adds color and contrast to many types of salads.

 Savoy cabbage has a looser head than other varieties and is very flavorful. The leaves have a "wrinkled" texture and range in color from dark green outer leaves to pale green inner leaves.

 Chinese or celery cabbage grows in a stalk and has pale green to white leaves that have many fine, prominent veins.

Spinach is a loose bunch of crisp dark green leaves that have a smooth surface. Young leaves are especially attractive due to their ruffled appearance.

Endive is commonly available in three varieties.

 Curly endive is a tight head of very curly leaves that are shaded from dark green at the outer edge to light green or yellow at the base or stalk. It has a slightly bitter flavor.

 Escarole is similar to curly endive but has broad flat leaves that are slightly curled toward the ends and is mild to bitter in flavor.

 Belgian endive (also called French endive or witloof) grows in a tight stalk and it also has elongated light green to white leaves. Although the flavor is pronounced, it is milder than curly endive or escarole.

Parsley is characterized by small, bright green, curly leaves that grow on long slim stems and by its pleasantly pungent flavor. It is used primarily as a garnish or as a seasoning for salads.

 Chives are a delicate member of the onion family. The leaves resemble long, very thin tubes and are dark green in color. Usually, they are finely chopped and used as a seasoning or garnish for salads.

 Watercress is grown in streams of clean running water. It has small bright green leaves that branch from slender stems. Watercress is a decorative garnish for almost any salad and can be added to tossed salads.

Other greens that are suitable for salads include turnip and mustard greens, chard, dandelion greens, celery leaves and cress.

Although most varieties of greens are available all year, there may be limited supplies at certain seasons of the year due to severe weather conditions.

An imaginative selection of greens and careful storage and preparation can make the difference between an ordinary and a great salad.

SALADS

A TOSS-UP

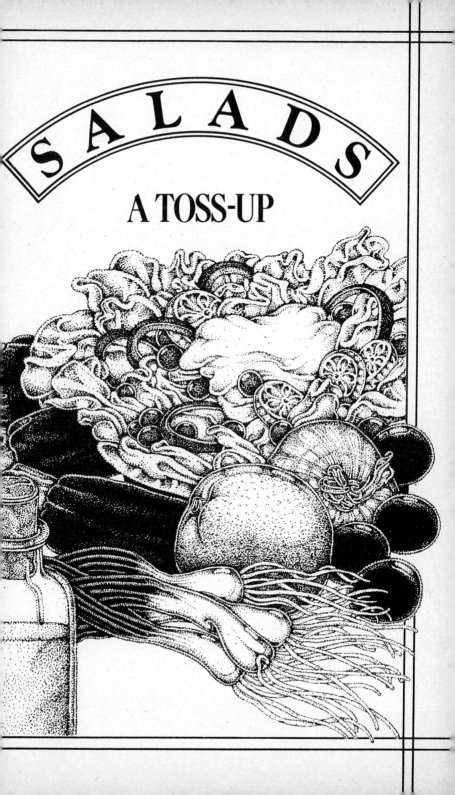

A tossed salad can be as simple as a bowl of assorted greens or as elaborate as a colorful combination of endive and exotic fruits. In America, tossed salads have been developed to a fine art and have become a mainstay of the daily diet. Depending on ingredients and size, these versatile salads can be served as appetizers, as main course accompaniments or main dishes. Greens are the characterizing ingredients in any tossed salad and contribute to the light, casual appearance.

In selecting ingredients, special consideration should be given to contrasts in color, flavor, texture and shape — and to a compatible dressing. To complement tossed salads, an extensive variety of convenient ready-to-serve dressings are available in any supermarket. Choosing the right dressing depends primarily on personal preference.

When possible, tossed salads should be prepared with chilled ingredients just before serving. Many or all of the ingredients can be prepared in advance and refrigerated in separate plastic bags or tightly covered containers, then tossed together at mealtime. Tossed salads can be completely prepared ahead of time, but must be tightly covered and refrigerated for no longer than two to three hours. The dressing should be served separately and added to the salad just before serving.

With a little imagination, it is easy to create salads that are colorful, appetizing and nutritious.

Cornucopia Salad

5 cups torn assorted greens
1 cup zucchini slices, cut
    in half
1 cup mushroom slices
1/2 cup carrot slices
1/2 cup pitted ripe olive slices

1 cup cherry tomato
    halves
Kraft thousand island
    or creamy Russian
    dressing

Combine greens, zucchini, mushrooms, carrot and olives; toss lightly. Top with tomato; serve with dressing.

8 servings

Zucchini Toss

1 1/2 qts. torn romaine
1 cup zucchini slices
3/4 cup radish slices
1/4 cup green onion slices
1/4 cup alfalfa sprouts

2 tablespoons Kraft
    grated parmesan cheese
1/4 cup Kraft Italian
    dressing

Combine romaine, zucchini, radishes, onion, alfalfa sprouts and cheese. Add dressing; toss lightly.

6 to 8 servings

Onion-Bibb Salad

1 qt. torn bibb lettuce
1 cup watercress
1 cup cucumber slices
1/2 cup onion rings
3 ozs. Kraft aged natural
    Swiss cheese, cut
    into chunks

1/2 teaspoon coarsely
    ground black pepper
Kraft red wine vinegar
    and oil dressing

Combine greens, cucumber, onion, cheese and pepper; toss lightly. Serve with dressing.

4 to 6 servings

Mock Caesar Salad

2 cups Italian bread cubes
Kraft Italian dressing
Kraft grated parmesan cheese
2 qts. torn romaine
2 cups iceberg lettuce chunks

1 cup red onion rings
2 hard-cooked eggs,
finely chopped
1/2 cup pitted ripe olives

Toss bread cubes with 3 tablespoons dressing and 2 tablespoons cheese; place on ungreased baking pan. Bake at 400°, 8 to 10 minutes or until lightly browned, stirring occasionally. Combine greens, onion, eggs and olives. Add 1/2 cup dressing; toss until greens are well coated. Add croutons and 1/3 cup cheese; toss lightly.

6 to 8 servings

All Seasons Salad

1 qt. torn assorted greens
1/2 cup cucumber slices
1/2 cup pitted ripe olives
1/4 cup radish slices

2 hard-cooked eggs, cut
into wedges
Kraft green onion
dressing

Combine greens, cucumber, olives and radishes; toss lightly. Top with eggs; serve with dressing.

4 servings

Winter Green Salad

1 1/2 qts. torn assorted greens
1 16-oz. jar crinkle cut
beets, drained
1 cup cooked peas

1/2 cup onion rings
Croutons
Kraft creamy cucumber
dressing

Combine greens, beets, peas and onion; toss lightly. Top with croutons; serve with dressing.

6 to 8 servings

Patio Salad

1 1/2 qts. torn iceberg lettuce
2 cups torn bibb lettuce
2 cups torn curly endive
2 cups shredded red cabbage
1 cup caulifloweret slices

1/2 cup celery slices
Kraft garlic French
dressing

Combine greens, cabbage, cauliflower and celery; toss lightly. Serve with dressing.

10 to 12 servings

Confetti Salad Slaw

2 qts. torn assorted greens
2 cups shredded red cabbage
1 1/2 cups cherry tomato halves
1 cup shredded carrots

1/2 cup chopped cucumber
Kraft thousand island
or creamy Russian
dressing

Combine greens, cabbage, tomato, carrot and cucumber; toss lightly. Serve with dressing.

8 to 10 servings

Wilted Lettuce Salad

3/4 cup Kraft oil and vinegar
dressing
2 qts. torn lettuce
8 crisply cooked bacon slices,
crumbled

1 cup red onion rings
2 hard-cooked eggs,
chopped

Heat dressing over low heat, stirring occasionally. Combine lettuce, bacon and onion. Add hot dressing; toss lightly. Top with eggs.

6 to 8 servings

This salad derives its name from its "wilted" appearance after being tossed with hot dressing.

Homespun Tossed Salad

1 1/2 qts. torn assorted greens
1 cup scored cucumber slices
1 cup cherry tomato halves
1 cup carrot curls
2 hard-cooked eggs, chopped

1/2 teaspoon dill weed
1 cup whole-wheat croutons
Kraft thousand island
or creamy Russian
dressing

Combine greens, cucumber, tomato, carrot, eggs and dill weed; toss lightly. Top with croutons; serve with dressing.

6 to 8 servings

Spinach Salad

1 qt. torn spinach
4 crisply cooked bacon slices,
crumbled

3 hard-cooked eggs, chopped
1/3 cup onion rings
Kraft Italian dressing

Combine spinach, bacon, eggs, onion and enough dressing to moisten; toss lightly.

6 to 8 servings

Sausalito Citrus Salad

2 qts. torn assorted greens
1 cup orange slices
1 cup whole-wheat croutons
1/2 cup chopped dates

1 tablespoon sesame
seed, toasted
Kraft French dressing

Combine greens, oranges, croutons, dates and sesame seed; toss lightly. Serve with dressing.

6 to 8 servings

Homespun Tossed Salad, Santa Maria Salad (page 22), Spinach Salad, Sausalito Citrus Salad

Santa Maria Salad

2 cups Italian bread cubes	2 cups caulifloweret slices
Kraft Italian dressing	2 cups broccoli flowerets
2 qts. torn assorted greens	1 1/2 cups zucchini slices

Toss bread cubes with 1/4 cup dressing; place on ungreased baking pan. Bake at 350°, 20 minutes, stirring occasionally. Combine croutons, 1/3 cup dressing, greens, cauliflower, broccoli and zucchini; toss lightly. Serve with additional dressing, if desired.

4 to 6 servings

Caesar Salad Roma

2 cups bread cubes	1 raw egg
Kraft Italian dressing	1/4 cup (1 oz.) Kraft
2 qts. torn assorted greens	grated parmesan cheese
1/2 cup onion rings	
1 tablespoon chopped anchovies	

Toss bread cubes with 1/4 cup dressing; place in ungreased baking pan. Bake at 350°, 20 minutes, stirring occasionally. Combine greens, onion and anchovies; toss lightly. Add 1/2 cup dressing and egg; toss until greens are well coated. Add croutons and cheese; toss lightly.

4 servings

Variation: For a main dish, add 6 1/2-oz. can tuna, drained, flaked.

Circus Salad

3 cups torn assorted greens	1/4 cup peanuts
1 1/2 cups apple slices	Catalina French
1/2 cup popcorn	dressing

Combine greens, apples, popcorn and peanuts; toss lightly. Serve with dressing.

4 servings

Pineapple Tossed Salad

1 qt. torn assorted greens
1 8-1/4-oz. can pineapple
　chunks, drained

1/2 cup shredded carrot
Kraft chunky blue
　cheese dressing

Combine greens, pineapple and carrot; toss lightly. Serve with dressing.

4 servings

Ham Salad Hawaiian

1 pineapple
1 qt. torn assorted greens
2 cups ham strips

1 cup celery slices
1/4 cup green onion slices
Catalina French dressing

Cut pineapple in half lengthwise through crown. Remove fruit, leaving shells intact. Core fruit; cut into chunks. Combine with greens, ham, celery and onion; toss lightly. Spoon into pineapple shells; serve with dressing.

2 servings

Chef's Secret Salad

1 8-oz. bottle Kraft thousand
　island or creamy Russian
　dressing
4 crisply cooked bacon slices,
　crumbled
2 tablespoons Kraft cold pack
　blue cheese, crumbled

1 1/2 qts. torn spinach
1 8-oz. jar crinkle cut
　beets, drained
1 cup scored cucumber
　slices
1 cup carrot curls
2/3 cup onion rings

Combine dressing, bacon and cheese; mix well. Chill. Combine remaining ingredients; toss lightly. Serve with dressing.

6 servings

Crumbled bacon and blue cheese add sophistication to this hearty vegetable salad.

Wilted Spinach Salad

1/3 cup Kraft oil and vinegar
    dressing
2 tablespoons finely chopped
    onion
1/4 teaspoon pepper
1 1/2 qts. torn spinach

4 crisply cooked bacon
    slices, crumbled
1/2 cup (2 ozs.) Kraft
    grated parmesan cheese
1 hard-cooked egg,
    chopped

Heat dressing, onion and pepper over low heat, stirring occasionally. Combine spinach, bacon and cheese. Add hot dressing; toss lightly. Top with egg.

6 servings

Crispy Apple Salad

2 raisin bread slices
2 qts. torn assorted greens
1 cup thin apple slices

1 cup cauliflowerets
1/2 cup celery slices
Kraft French dressing

Cut bread into cubes; place on ungreased baking pan. Bake at 350°, 10 minutes or until golden brown. Combine croutons, greens, apples, cauliflower and celery; toss lightly. Serve with dressing.

8 to 10 servings

Marinated Vegetable Toss

1 8-oz. bottle Kraft Italian
    dressing
2 cups cauliflowerets,
    partially cooked, drained
2 cups carrot slices,
    partially cooked, drained

1 cucumber, sliced
1 qt. shredded lettuce

Pour dressing over combined cauliflower, carrot and cucumber. Cover; marinate in refrigerator several hours. Drain, reserving marinade. Combine vegetables and lettuce; toss lightly. Serve with marinade.

8 servings

Fiesta Salad Bowl

1 8-oz. bottle Catalina
French dressing
1 15-1/2-oz. can garbanzo
beans
1/2 cup cucumber slices

1/2 cup caulifloweret slices
1/2 cup green pepper strips
1/2 cup pitted ripe olives
2 qts. torn assorted
greens

Pour dressing over beans, cucumber, cauliflower, green pepper and olives. Cover; marinate in refrigerator several hours. Drain, reserving marinade. Combine vegetables and greens; toss lightly. Serve with marinade.

6 to 8 servings

A colorful tossed salad with that south-of-the-border flavor.

Citrus Salad Bowl

1/2 cup Kraft oil and vinegar
dressing
1/4 cup orange juice
1/2 teaspoon poppy seed
1/4 teaspoon grated
orange rind

2 cups torn spinach
2 cups torn bibb lettuce
1 cup grapefruit sections
1/2 cup orange slices
1 cup red onion rings

Combine dressing, orange juice, poppy seed and orange rind; mix well. Combine greens, fruit and onion; toss lightly. Serve with dressing.

4 to 6 servings

Cucumber Fruit Salad

2 qts. torn assorted greens
2 cups cantaloupe chunks
1 1/2 cups strawberry halves
1 11-oz. can mandarin orange
segments, drained

Kraft creamy cucumber
dressing

Combine greens and fruit; toss lightly. Serve with dressing.

8 servings

Frontier Salad Toss

1 8-oz. bottle Kraft French
    dressing
2 teaspoons chili powder
2 qts. torn assorted greens

2 cups tomato wedges
1 12-oz. can mexicorn,
    drained
Shoestring potatoes

Combine dressing and chili powder; mix well. Combine greens, tomato and corn; toss lightly. Top with potatoes; serve with dressing.

8 servings

Copenhagen Vegetable Salad

1 qt. torn spinach
1 16-oz. jar sliced beets,
    drained
1/2 cup onion rings

3 hard-cooked eggs, cut
    into wedges
Roka brand blue cheese
    dressing

Combine spinach, beets and onion; toss lightly. Top with eggs; serve with dressing.

6 to 8 servings

Far East Salad

1 1/2 qts. torn spinach
1 hard-cooked egg, chopped
1 16-oz. can bean sprouts,
    drained
1 8-oz. can bamboo shoots,
    drained

2 tablespoons sesame
    seed, toasted
Kraft oil and vinegar
    dressing

Combine spinach and egg; toss lightly. Arrange bean sprouts and bamboo shoots on spinach mixture; sprinkle with sesame seed. Serve with dressing.

6 servings

Frontier Salad Toss

Grapefruit Tossed Salad

1 qt. torn romaine
2 cups torn bibb lettuce
2 cups grapefruit segments
1 cup red onion rings

4 crisply cooked bacon
  slices, crumbled
Kraft French dressing

Combine greens, grapefruit, onion and bacon; toss lightly. Serve with dressing.

6 servings

Mexican Fiesta Salad

1 1/2 qts. torn lettuce
1 avocado, peeled, chopped
4 tomatoes, chopped
1 green pepper, chopped
1 small onion, chopped

Miracle brand French
  dressing
4 crisply cooked bacon
  slices, crumbled

Combine lettuce, avocado, tomato, green pepper, onion and enough dressing to moisten; toss lightly. Sprinkle with bacon.

6 to 8 servings

South Pacific Salad

1 head iceberg lettuce, cut
  into 1-inch chunks
1 11-oz. can mandarin orange
  segments, drained
1 8-1/4-oz. can pineapple
  chunks, drained

1/2 cup chopped green pepper
1/4 cup chopped peanuts
Catalina French
  dressing

Combine lettuce, orange segments, pineapple, green pepper and nuts with enough dressing to moisten; toss lightly.

6 servings

SALADS

THE SEASON'S BEST VEGETABLES

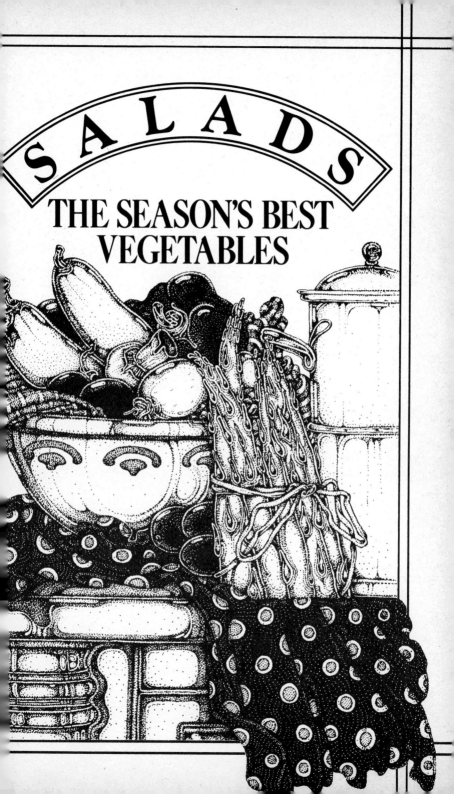

Vegetables are primary salad ingredients valued for their varied flavors, bright colors, crisp textures and interesting shapes. Vegetables grow on different parts of plants which explains their varied shapes.

- **Roots** include potatoes, carrots, onions and turnips.
- **Stems** include celery and asparagus.
- **Leaves** include lettuce, cabbage, watercress and parsley.
- **Flowers** include cauliflower and broccoli.
- **Seeds** include peas and corn.
- **Fruits** include tomatoes and green peppers.

Fortunately, many fresh vegetables are available in most parts of the country all year long. When favorite vegetables are not available in the fresh produce section of the supermarket, investigate the canned and frozen alternatives.

Selection and Care

High quality, flavorful vegetables are more plentiful and lower priced when purchased in season. When shopping, look for fresh vegetables which are blemish free. Proper size, shape and color are your clues to selecting vegetables that are at their peak eating quality. Choose those that look good enough to eat raw. Root vegetables, such as carrots, should be bought without their tops, unless the tops are also going to be used.

Most fresh vegetables are lightly washed and gently dried before being stored in the refrigerator. However, root vegetables such as potatoes, carrots, onions, squash and turnips are stored unwashed in a cool, dark, well-ventilated area. A good rule to follow: store vegetables in the same way they were stored in the supermarket. Always check the labels of canned or frozen products for storage directions.

Preparation Tips

A few easy techniques make vegetable preparation simpler and salads more attractive.

Scoring Cucumber or Zucchini — Run tines of a fork lengthwise along the unpeeled vegetable.

Coring Lettuce — Whack core-end of lettuce on a counter, then lift or twist out core. Core may also be cut out with a knife, but cut edges discolor more quickly.

Cauliflowerets — Separate cauliflower head into small buds.

Broccoli Flowerets — Separate stalk of broccoli into small buds.

Specialty Vegetables

Here is a varied selection of novel vegetables which can add new interest to salads.

Alfalfa Sprouts are creamy white filaments tipped with tiny green leaves. Sprouts have a fresh, earthy flavor and are high in protein. Sprinkle on tossed or arranged salads for a decorative garnish and added crunch.

Artichokes are the leafy buds from a plant resembling thistle. Eat the tender part of the leaves by drawing the leaves between your teeth. Remove the prickly choke and eat the delicate heart with a fork.

Bean Sprouts are crisp tendrils that have a fresh delicate flavor. Cooked or raw they add a crunchy texture to tossed, mixed or hot salads.

Bok Choy forms a head of dark green leaves with firm white stems and is often topped with a pale yellow flower. Bok choy has a slightly sweet flavor, which is stronger than Chinese cabbage. Use it sliced, chopped or torn in salads. Bok choy is available all year.

Broccoli has dark green clusters of flower buds on a thick green stem. It is a close relative to cauliflower and one of the richest sources of vitamin C. Use broccoli flowers and stems, raw or partially cooked, in vegetable or main dish salads.

Garbanzo Beans (or chick peas) have an irregular shape, firm texture and a nut-like flavor. These peas are widely used in Spanish-American cuisines and are an excellent protein source. Garbanzos are available fresh or canned all year.

Jicama is a brownish root which resembles turnips. When peeled, it has a crisp texture and mild flavor similar to water chestnuts, for which it is an inexpensive alternate.

Snow Peas (or sugar peas) are shaped like a flat, broad pea pod. The pods have a delicate flavor and crisp texture and are used in many oriental dishes. Add them to accompaniment or main dish salads. Available all year fresh or frozen.

Water Chestnuts have a creamy white, crisp flesh and a chestnut-brown skin. Their flavor is often described as "chestnutty." Often used raw, they have a unique ability to remain crisp and crunchy after cooking.

Zucchini is a variety of summer squash which is cylindrical in shape with smooth, thin, dark green skin. Its pale green flesh has a fresh delicate flavor. Slice, cube or shred for salads.

VEGETABLE	PEAK SEASON	QUALITY CHARACTERISTICS
Alfalfa Sprouts	All year	Fresh appearance, crisp
Artichokes	April-May	Heavy for size, compact leaves, plump, fresh, green color
Asparagus	March-June	Firm, compact tips
Beans	June-September	Fresh, clean appearance; tender; crisp; reasonably well-shaped
Bean Sprouts	All year	Fresh, crisp, moist tips
Beets	June-October	Smooth firm body, globular shape
Broccoli	October-May	Firm, compact stalk with small flower buds; bright color
Brussels Sprouts	October-March	Firm, compact, fresh, green color
Cabbage	All year	Firm solid head, heavy for size
Carrots	All year	Firm, smooth, well-shaped, bright orange
Cauliflower	October-November	Firm, compact head; white or creamy white; fresh, green leaves
Celery	All year	Crisp, clean stalks; light green with glossy surface
Chilies	All year	Irregular shape; bright, shiny skins
Corn	May-August	Green husks, silk ends free from decay, plump kernels
Cucumbers	May-July	Fairly firm, waxy skin, uniform color
Green Onions	May-July	Firm white tops; slender, green stems
Jicama	November-June	Firm, thin brown skin resembles turnip

VEGETABLE	PEAK SEASON	QUALITY CHARACTERISTICS
Leeks	All year	Bright green tops, firm white bulbs, bright green stems
Mushrooms	All year	Clean, creamy color
Okra	May-October	Crisp, bright green pods; small to medium-sized
Onions	All year	Firm, dry, outer surfaces covered with papery skin
Peas	April-July	Firm, bright green pods; velvety to the touch
Peppers	All year	Firm, well-formed, thick-fleshed, bright color
Potatoes	All year	Firm, smooth, reasonably well-shaped
Radishes	March-May	Well-formed, smooth, firm, crisp
Rhubarb	February-June	Firm, crisp, tender stalks
Shallots	All year	Fresh green tops; young, crisp, tender necks
Summer Squash	All year	Fairly heavy for size, lustrous surface, firm
Tomatoes	May-August	Plump, well-shaped, free from blemishes, uniform red color
Turnips	October-March	Firm, smooth, few fibrous roots at base
Water Chestnuts	All year	Very firm, chestnut-brown skins

Piquant Potato Salad (page 36), Pennsylvania Pepper Slaw (page 36)

Piquant Potato Salad

1 1/2 qts. chopped cooked potatoes
1 1/2 cups celery slices
1/2 cup radish slices
1/2 cup chopped onion
1/4 cup chopped green pepper
2 hard-cooked eggs, chopped

Kraft thousand island
  or creamy Russian
  dressing
Salt and pepper

Combine vegetables, eggs and enough dressing to moisten; mix lightly. Season to taste. Chill. Add additional dressing before serving, if desired. Garnish with hard-cooked egg wedges and parsley, if desired.

10 to 12 servings

Pennsylvania Pepper Slaw

1 1/2 qts. shredded cabbage
1 cup chopped red and green
  pepper
1 cup celery slices

1/2 cup Kraft Italian
  dressing
1 tablespoon brown sugar
1 teaspoon celery seed

Combine cabbage, pepper and celery. Add combined dressing, sugar and celery seed; mix lightly. Chill. Toss again just before serving. Garnish with pepper rings, if desired.

6 to 8 servings

A traditional sweet-tart coleslaw with the added zest of Italian dressing.

Bacon, Lettuce And Tomato Salad

6 bacon slices
1 qt. shredded lettuce

Kraft coleslaw dressing
1 1/2 cups tomato slices

Cut bacon slices into quarters; cook until crisp. Combine lettuce and enough dressing to moisten; toss lightly. Arrange tomato on individual salad plates; top with lettuce and bacon.

4 servings

This salad combines the ingredients of the ever-popular "BLT" sandwich in a crisp, flavorful salad. It is an excellent accompaniment salad.

Stack-Up Salad

2 cups shredded lettuce
1 1/2 cups shredded carrots
1 1/2 cups shredded zucchini

Kraft creamy cucumber
dressing

Layer lettuce, carrot and zucchini on individual salad plates. Serve with dressing.

4 to 6 servings

Variation: Top with alfalfa sprouts.

Peas 'N Cheese Salad

1 10-oz. pkg. frozen peas,
thawed
1 cup (4 ozs.) cubed Kraft
mild natural colby cheese
1/2 cup celery slices

1/2 cup shredded carrot
1/3 cup Kraft French
dressing
Lettuce

Combine peas, cheese, celery, carrot and dressing; mix lightly. Serve on lettuce-covered plates. Serve with additional dressing, if desired.

6 servings

Creamy Garlic Potato Salad

1 qt. chopped cooked potatoes
1 cup celery slices
1/3 cup pitted ripe olive slices
2 hard-cooked eggs, chopped
2 tablespoons green onion
slices

1/2 teaspoon salt
1/4 teaspoon pepper
1/2 cup Kraft creamy
garlic dressing

Combine ingredients; mix lightly. Chill several hours. Add additional dressing before serving, if desired.

6 servings

A hearty accompaniment salad for baked chicken, roast beef or ham sandwiches.

Vegetable Potpourri Salad

1 cup dairy sour cream
3/4 cup Kraft coleslaw dressing
1/2 teaspoon curry powder
1 qt. shredded lettuce
1 1/2 cups cucumber slices,
    cut in half

1 cup red onion rings
2 10-oz. pkgs. frozen
    peas, cooked, drained
2 crisply cooked bacon
    slices, crumbled

Combine sour cream, dressing and curry powder; mix well. Chill. In 2 1/2-quart bowl, layer lettuce, cucumber, onion and peas. Chill. Garnish with bacon; serve with dressing.

8 servings

Bavarian Beet Salad

1 cup chopped cucumber
1 cup onion rings
1/2 teaspoon dill weed
1/2 teaspoon salt
1/8 teaspoon pepper
1 16-oz. jar sliced beets,
    drained

Lettuce
Kraft thousand island
    or creamy Russian
    dressing

Combine cucumber, onion and seasonings; mix lightly. Chill. Arrange beets on lettuce-covered platter; top with cucumber mixture. Serve with dressing.

4 to 6 servings

Marinated Napoli Salad

1 8-oz. bottle Kraft Italian
    dressing
3 tomatoes, sliced
1 1/2 cups zucchini slices

1 1/2 cups mushroom slices
1/4 cup chopped parsley
2 qts. shredded lettuce

Pour dressing over tomato, zucchini, mushrooms and parsley. Cover; marinate in refrigerator several hours. Drain, reserving marinade. Arrange vegetables on lettuce-covered platter. Serve with marinade.

8 to 10 servings

Vegetable Potpourri Salad, Bavarian Beet Salad, Marinated Napoli Salad

California Skewer Salad

1 cup caulifloweret slices
1 cup mushrooms
1 cup cherry tomatoes
1 cup broccoli flowerets
1 head iceberg lettuce, cut
   into 6 wedges

Kraft thousand island
  or creamy Russian
  dressing

Alternate cauliflower, mushrooms, tomato and broccoli on skewers; insert in lettuce. Serve with dressing.

6 servings

Cheesy Cucumber Salad

2 cups cucumber slices
2 cups chopped apples
1/4 cup Kraft creamy cucumber
   dressing

Lettuce
1/4 cup (1 oz.) shredded
  Kraft sharp natural
  cheddar cheese

Combine cucumber, apples and dressing; mix lightly. Serve on lettuce-covered plate; sprinkle with cheese. Serve with additional dressing, if desired.

4 servings

Normandy Lettuce Salad

1 head iceberg lettuce
1/2 cup Roka brand blue cheese
   dressing
1 8-oz. pkg. Philadelphia
   Brand cream cheese

1 cup broccoli flowerets
1/2 cup radish slices

Remove center of lettuce, leaving 1-inch shell. Gradually add dressing to softened cream cheese, mixing until well blended. Add broccoli and radishes to cream cheese mixture; mix lightly. Fill lettuce shell with cream cheese mixture. Cover; chill overnight. Cut into slices or wedges to serve.

6 servings

These filled lettuce wedges are ideal first course or luncheon salads. For a simple and equally attractive alternate, spoon the dressing mixture over lettuce wedges.

Aztec Salad

1 12-oz. can whole kernel
corn, drained
1 8-oz. can kidney beans,
drained
1/2 cup chopped onion
1/3 cup chopped green pepper

1/4 cup Catalina French
dressing
2 tablespoons chopped
pimiento
8 avocado halves, peeled

Combine corn, beans, onion, green pepper, dressing and pimiento; mix lightly. Chill. Place avocados on platter; fill with vegetable mixture.

8 servings

Starburst Salad

1 cup dairy sour cream
1/2 cup Kraft Italian dressing
2 cups carrot slices,
partially cooked
1 1/2 cups zucchini slices

1 cup mushroom slices
1/2 cup pitted ripe olive
slices
1 head iceberg lettuce,
cut into 6 wedges

Combine sour cream and dressing; mix well. Chill. Combine carrot, zucchini, mushrooms and olives; mix lightly. Spoon over lettuce. Serve with dressing.

6 servings

Vegetable Salad Plate

1 8-oz. bottle Kraft golden
blend Italian dressing
1 10-oz. pkg. frozen asparagus
spears, thawed, drained

1 cup caulifloweret slices
1/2 cup carrot slices
2 tomatoes, sliced
4 iceberg lettuce slices

Pour dressing over asparagus, cauliflower, carrot and tomato. Cover; marinate in refrigerator several hours or overnight. Drain, reserving marinade. Arrange vegetables on lettuce-covered plates. Serve with marinade.

4 servings

An attractive and colorfully arranged salad that can be prepared several hours in advance, then covered and refrigerated until serving.

Roadside Ratatouille

1 16-oz. can whole green
beans, drained
1 1/2 cups cherry tomato halves
1 1/2 cups cauliflowerets,
cooked, drained

1 1/2 cups mushroom slices
1 cup onion rings
2/3 cup Catalina French
dressing

Combine ingredients; mix lightly. Chill. Serve in lettuce-lined bowl, if desired.

8 servings

Sunset Salad

1 8-oz. bottle Kraft Italian
dressing
1 8-1/2-oz. can artichoke
hearts, drained, quartered

12 tomato slices
1/2 cup green pepper chunks
1 avocado, peeled, sliced
Lettuce

Pour dressing over artichoke hearts, tomato and green pepper. Cover; marinate in refrigerator several hours. Drain, reserving marinade. Arrange tomato and avocado in pinwheel design on lettuce-covered plate; top with artichoke hearts and green pepper. Serve with marinade.

4 servings

Chunky Garden Salad

1 cup plain yogurt
1/2 cup Kraft Italian dressing
2 cups cherry tomato halves

1 1/2 cups cucumber chunks
1 cup thick celery slices
1/2 cup radish slices

Combine yogurt and dressing; mix well. Chill. Combine vegetables; mix lightly. Chill. Serve with dressing.

6 servings

SALADS
THE SEASON'S BEST FRUITS

Few salad ingredients are as flavorful and attractive as fresh fruits. They make a bright addition to any salad and are a colorful contrast in slaws and mixed greens.

Each season offers a variety of fresh fruits for salad making, but when your favorites are out-of-season, explore the many canned, frozen and dried fruits available all year long. Occasionally, substitute less familiar fruits for the frequently used favorites.

Fruit salads are perfect for many parts of the meal. Compotes and arranged fruit platters, for example, make ideal appetizers. Tossed salads, coleslaw and the many variations of Waldorf salad are popular accompaniment salads. Fruits paired with a protein food, such as chicken or tuna salad in a cantaloupe half, provide a hearty, main dish salad.

Selection and Care

Fruits, with their wide variety of colors and flavors, are a favorite salad ingredient. Fortunately, several popular fresh fruits, such as apples and bananas, are available for salad making throughout the year. Many fruits, however, are in peak supply during certain months of the year. Fresh fruits purchased during these seasons are generally more flavorful and less expensive.

When selecting fresh fruits, handle them carefully to prevent injury. Look for firm and unblemished fruits. Citrus fruits, pineapples and melons should be heavy for their size. Apples and oranges are best purchased at full maturity. Bananas, peaches, pears, melons and pineapples can be ripened at home by leaving them at room temperature in a loosely closed bag or a fruit bowl.

To prevent spoilage, buy only as much fruit as you need and store ripened fruit in a cool, dry place or in the refrigerator. Fresh fruit should be thoroughly washed before salad preparation, but not soaked, since some of the flavor and the nutrients may be lost. When preparing fresh apples, pears, bananas and avocados for salads, brush the cut surfaces with citrus juice to prevent discoloring. Because fresh fruit is highly perishable, it must always be handled carefully.

Special Preparation Techniques

Some fruits require a little extra attention or special preparation when used in salads.

Pitting an Avocado — Cut ripe avocado in half lengthwise around pit; twist halves slightly to separate. To remove pit, strike with sharp edge of knife; twist and lift out. Carefully peel off skin and cut avocado into desired shapes. Dip in citrus juice to prevent discoloring.

Cracking a Coconut — Using a hammer, tap an imaginary line around middle of coconut until it splits in half. Remove coconut meat by slipping knife between meat and shell. Finely chop, shred or grate the meat.

Slicing Kiwi Fruit — Chill fruit; rub off fuzzy part of skin and carefully peel. Slice with a utility or paring knife.

Sectioning an Orange — Run sharp knife between membrane and orange section, cutting to center of orange; twist blade and separate fruit from membrane on opposite side; remove section.

Pears, Apples and Bananas — To prevent discoloring, dip cut fruit in citrus juice before using in salads.

Specialty Fruits

Less familiar fruits provide intriguing shapes, colors and flavors that add a gourmet touch to salads.

Avocado varies in skin texture and color ranging from green to black, depending on the area where it is grown. Avocado halves make perfect shells for holding a variety of salad mixtures.

Kiwi Fruit is oval-shaped with fuzzy brown skin. The meat is a beautiful lime green with tiny, edible black seeds. Flavor is a cross between strawberries, bananas and watermelon. Peel and slice to use in salads.

Mango is elongated or almost round. The skin may be green, yellow or tinged with red or yellow, depending on the variety. To use in salads, score the skin, peel, and slice or chunk the fruit.

Papaya is pear-shaped with a smooth green to yellow skin, golden meat and shiny black seeds. Flavor is a cross between a peach and a cantaloupe. Cut papaya in half, remove seeds, peel, and slice or chunk to use in salads.

FRUIT	PEAK SEASON	QUALITY CHARACTERISTICS
Apples	All year	Firm, bright color for variety
Apricots	June-July	Fairly firm, plump, well-formed, uniform color
Avocados	All year	Fairly firm, yields to slight pressure on outer rind, heavy for size
Bananas	All year	Firm, unblemished, bright yellow color
Blueberries	June-August	Plump, uniform size and color, clean, dry, free of leaves and stems
Cantaloupes	June-August	Well-netted rind, slightly soft at stem end, well-formed, fragrant
Casaba Melons	September-October	Smooth yellow rind, slightly soft at stem end
Cherries	May-July	Firm, plump, uniform color
Coconuts	September-April	Heavy for size, use "slosh test" to insure that coconut has milk
Cranberries	September-December	Firm, plump, uniform color, lustrous
Crenshaw Melons	August-September	Golden rind, slightly soft at stem end, fragrant
Dates	All year	Soft, lustrous brown color, slightly wrinkled skin
Figs	June-October	Fairly soft, pear-shaped, color depends on variety
Grapefruit	January-April	Fairly firm, plump, well-formed, heavy for size, uniform color
Grapes	July-November	Plump, firmly attached to stem, lustrous color

FRUIT	PEAK SEASON	QUALITY CHARACTERISTICS
Honeydew Melons	June-October	Plump, slightly soft at stem end
Kiwis	June-March	Slightly soft, uniform size
Lemons	All year	Plump, heavy for size, fine-textured rind, uniform color
Limes	All year	Plump, heavy for size, fine-textured rind, bright green
Mangoes	May-August	Fairly firm, smooth skin, bright color
Nectarines	June-September	Plump, slightly soft, bright uniform color
Oranges	December-May	Firm, heavy for size, fine-textured rind, uniform color
Papayas	May-June & October-December	Fairly firm, smooth yellow skin
Peaches	July-August	Fairly firm, free of blemishes, bright fresh appearance
Pears	August-November	Fairly firm, free from bruises
Pineapples	March-June	Firm, plump, heavy for size, yellow to green color, fragrant
Plums	July-August	Fairly firm to slightly soft, smooth skin, uniform color
Raspberries	June-July	Plump, velvety appearance, bright uniform color
Strawberries	April-June	Fairly firm, uniform red color
Tangelos	November-January	Firm, coarse textured skin, bright orange color
Tangerines	November-January	Small, heavy for size, coarse shiny skin
Watermelons	June-August	Firm, heavy, symmetrical, yellowish underside

Fun Fruit Faces

2 cups shredded carrots
1 1/2 cups celery slices
1 cup raisins
1/2 cup peanuts
1/2 cup Kraft coleslaw dressing

1 29-oz. can pear or
    peach halves, drained
Lettuce
Kraft miniature
    marshmallows

Combine carrots, celery, raisins, nuts and dressing; mix well. Chill. Arrange fruit and slaw mixture on lettuce-covered plates. Make faces using additional raisins, nuts, celery or marshmallows.

8 servings

Making faces on peach or pear halves is fun and easy when Mom has help in the kitchen.

Sunny Citrus Salad

3/4 cup Kraft French dressing
3 tablespoons chutney
1 16-oz. jar Kraft pure
    chilled unsweetened
    grapefruit sections

1 11-oz. can mandarin
    orange segments,
    drained
1 cup avocado chunks

Combine dressing and chutney; mix well. Combine fruit; mix lightly. Serve with dressing.

4 servings

Sunshine Salad Toss

1 1/2 qts. torn assorted greens
1 8-1/4-oz. can pineapple
    chunks, drained
1 cup scored cucumber slices

1 cup chopped pitted dates
1/2 cup shredded carrot
Kraft French or chunky
    blue cheese dressing

Combine ingredients; toss lightly. Serve with dressing.

6 to 8 servings

Dates can be pitted by making a lengthwise slit in the fruit and removing the pit. Chop dates with kitchen shears or a sharp knife that has been dipped in water to prevent sticking.

Breakfast Citrus Cups

4 grapefruit
2 cups grape halves
2 cups orange sections

1/2 cup natural wheat and
   barley cereal
Catalina French dressing

Cut grapefruit in half. Remove sections and membrane, leaving shells intact. Combine grapefruit sections, grapes and oranges; mix lightly. Chill. Add cereal to fruit mixture just before serving. Spoon fruit mixture into grapefruit shells; serve with dressing.

8 servings

Summer Spinach Salad

1/2 cup Kraft coleslaw dressing
2 tablespoons honey
1 teaspoon grated orange rind
1 qt. torn spinach
2 large bananas, sliced

3 crisply cooked bacon
   slices, crumbled
1/2 cup coarsely choppped
   walnuts

Combine dressing, honey and orange rind; mix well. Combine spinach, bananas, bacon and nuts; toss lightly. Serve with dressing.

4 servings

Harvest Salad

1 qt. shredded lettuce
2 cups chopped apples
1 cup shredded carrots
2 bananas, sliced

1/2 cup raisins
1/2 cup Kraft coleslaw
   dressing

Combine ingredients; toss lightly.

6 servings

Rainbow Melon Salad

1 cup orange sherbet
1/2 cup Kraft coleslaw dressing
   Honeydew or crenshaw melon
   Grapes

Apple chunks
Cantaloupe balls
Banana chunks

Combine sherbet and dressing; mix well. Chill. Cut melon in half horizontally; remove seeds. Scoop out melon balls, leaving shells intact. Cut zigzag pattern 1 inch deep around top of shell. Combine fruit; mix lightly. Spoon into melon shells; serve with dressing.

Pineapple Salad Bowl

1/4 cup Kraft chunky blue
   cheese dressing
1 tablespoon sugar
1/2 cup heavy cream, whipped
1 fresh pineapple
2 bananas, sliced

1 cup orange segments
1/2 cup strawberry halves
1/2 cup blueberries
2 tablespoons chopped
   walnuts, toasted

Combine dressing and sugar; mix well. Fold in whipped cream. Chill. Cut pineapple in half lengthwise through crown. Remove fruit, leaving shells intact. Core fruit; cut into chunks. Combine with bananas, oranges, strawberries and blueberries; mix lightly. Spoon into pineapple shells; top with dressing. Garnish with nuts.

2 servings

California Avocado Refresher

1 cup watermelon balls
1 cup cantaloupe balls
1/2 cup honeydew melon chunks
1/2 cup celery slices
4 avocado halves, peeled

Lettuce
2 tablespoons Kraft cold
   pack blue cheese,
   crumbled
Kraft French dressing

Combine melon and celery; mix lightly. Place avocados on individual lettuce-covered plates; fill with fruit mixture. Top with cheese; serve with dressing.

4 servings

Rainbow Melon Salad, Pineapple Salad Bowl, California Avocado Refresher

Fresno Fruit Salad

1 8-oz. bottle Kraft French
  dressing
1/4 cup honey
1/4 teaspoon ground coriander
1 1/2 qts. torn spinach

1 cup pear slices
1 cup peach slices
1 cup grape halves
1/4 cup alfalfa sprouts

Combine dressing, honey and coriander; mix well. Combine spinach, fruit and alfalfa sprouts; toss lightly. Serve with dressing.

6 to 8 servings

Waldorf Salad Platter

3 cups chopped apples
1 cup red grape halves
1 cup Kraft miniature
  marshmallows
1/2 cup celery slices

1/2 cup walnut halves,
  toasted
1/3 cup Kraft coleslaw
  dressing
1 qt. shredded lettuce

Combine fruit, marshmallows, celery, nuts and dressing; mix lightly. Arrange on lettuce-covered platter; serve with additional dressing, if desired.

6 servings

This version of the classic Waldorf salad combines the traditional ingredients of apples, celery and nuts with shredded lettuce, marshmallows and grapes.

California Sundae

1 cup pear slices
1 cup nectarine slices
1 cup plum slices
1 cup peach slices

2 cups cottage cheese
2 tablespoons chopped
  walnuts, toasted
Kraft French dressing

Arrange fruit in individual dessert dishes. Top each serving with 1/2 cup cottage cheese; sprinkle with nuts. Serve with dressing.

4 servings

Fresno Fruit Salad

Cantaloupe Onion Salad

1/2 cup Kraft oil and
    vinegar dressing
1/4 cup orange juice
1/2 teaspoon poppy seed
1/4 teaspoon grated orange rind

4 cups cantaloupe chunks
1 cup onion rings
6 crisply cooked bacon
    slices, crumbled
Lettuce

Combine dressing, orange juice, poppy seed and orange rind; mix well. Combine 1/4 cup dressing, cantaloupe, onion and bacon; mix lightly. Serve on lettuce-covered plates with remaining dressing.

8 servings

Florentine Citrus Salad

2/3 cup Kraft French dressing
1/3 cup Kraft chopped blue
    cheese crumbles
2 teaspoons celery seed
2 1/2 qts. torn assorted greens

1/2 cup onion rings
1/2 cup orange sections
1/2 cup grapefruit sections
1/2 cup celery slices
1/2 cup walnut halves

Combine dressing, cheese and celery seed; mix well. Chill. Combine greens, onion, orange and grapefruit sections, celery and nuts; toss lightly. Serve with dressing.

10 servings

Fanciful Fruit Platter

4 bananas, cut into 1-inch
    pieces
2/3 cup Roka brand blue
    cheese dressing
3/4 cup shredded coconut,
    toasted

2 cups grapes
1 11-oz. can mandarin
    orange segments
1 cup strawberries
1 8-1/4-oz. can pineapple
    chunks, drained

Dip bananas in dressing; coat with coconut. Arrange bananas and remaining fruit on platter. Garnish with mint and serve with additional dressing, if desired.

8 servings

SALADS

PRIMARILY FROM THE PANTRY

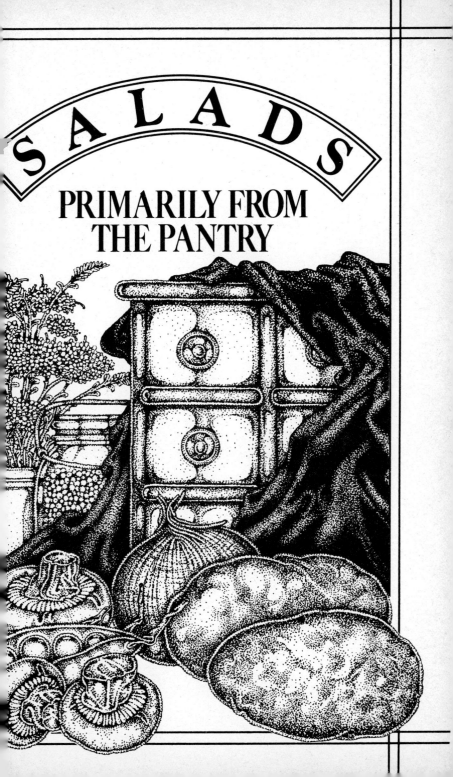

Unexpected guests appear! There's no time to shop! You're snowbound! Fresh produce is currently out of season and expensive! With a substantial stock of reliable staples, you can conquer these emergencies with confidence and ease. A few choice ingredients from the freezer, refrigerator or pantry can be the beginning of a sensational salad.

A quick survey might reveal a can of beans, corn, peaches, pineapple, tuna or luncheon meat; a pasta dinner or rice; herbs and spices; a few root vegetables; and several favorite dressings — enough variety for several creative combinations. Put your imagination to work and select a salad from the following appetizing selections.

Cucumber-Mac Salad

1 7-1/4-oz. pkg. Kraft macaroni
    and cheese dinner
1 cup cottage cheese
3/4 cup chopped cucumber
1/2 cup chopped onion
1/4 cup chopped parsley
1/4 cup chopped pimiento
1/2 cup Kraft creamy
    cucumber dressing
Red pepper rings
Cucumber slices

Prepare dinner as directed on package. Add cottage cheese, cucumber, onion, parsley, pimiento and dressing; mix lightly. Chill. Add additional dressing before serving, if desired. Garnish with red pepper and cucumber.

6 to 8 servings

Kraft macaroni and cheese dinner teamed with cottage cheese makes a nutritious main dish salad.

Three Bean Salad

1 16-oz. can cut green beans, drained
1 16-oz. can lima beans, drained
1 16-oz. can kidney beans, drained
1 cup chopped tomato
1 cup celery slices
1/2 cup chopped sweet pickle
Kraft French or Catalina French dressing

Combine vegetables, pickle and enough dressing to moisten; mix lightly. Chill.

10 to 12 servings

Rhode Island Relish

1 16-oz. can cut green beans, drained
1 12-oz. can whole kernel corn, drained
1/2 cup Kraft oil and vinegar dressing
1/2 cup celery slices
2 tablespoons chopped pimiento
Lettuce
4 crisply cooked bacon slices, crumbled

Combine beans, corn, dressing, celery and pimiento; mix lightly. Chill. Spoon into lettuce-lined bowl; sprinkle with bacon.

6 to 8 servings

Pantry Potato Salad

1 32-oz. pkg. frozen small whole potatoes
1 10-oz. pkg. frozen peas, thawed, drained
1 cup celery slices
3/4 cup Kraft creamy Italian dressing
1/4 cup chopped cherry peppers
1/2 teaspoon salt

Place potatoes in 1 quart boiling water. Bring to boil; simmer 10 minutes or until tender. Slice potatoes; chill. Combine potatoes and remaining ingredients; mix lightly. Chill several hours. Add additional dressing before serving, if desired. Garnish with cherry peppers.

8 servings

Confetti Kidney Bean Salad

1 16-oz. can kidney beans,
   drained
2/3 cup shredded carrot
1/2 cup chopped green pepper
4 hard-cooked eggs, chopped

1/4 cup chopped onion
1/2 cup Kraft thousand
   island or creamy
   Russian dressing
Lettuce

Combine beans, carrot, green pepper, eggs, onion and dressing; mix lightly. Chill. Serve on lettuce.

4 to 6 servings

Ham 'N Rice Salad

3/4 cup Kraft golden blend
   Italian dressing
1 10-oz. pkg. frozen peas,
   thawed, drained
1/2 cup red onion rings
1 4-oz. can mushrooms, drained

2 tablespoons chopped
   pimiento
2 cups cooked rice
1 1/2 cups ham strips
Lettuce

Pour dressing over peas, onion, mushrooms and pimiento. Cover; marinate in refrigerator several hours or overnight. Drain. Combine vegetables, rice and ham; mix lightly. Arrange on lettuce-covered platter. Garnish with pimiento or onion rings, if desired.

4 servings

This flavorful salad combination can be easily prepared in advance with leftover ham and rice.

Sunny Date Salad

1 1/2 qts. torn curly endive
1 16-oz. can peach slices
1 cup pitted dates, halved

1/2 cup bite-size crispy
   wheat squares
Kraft Russian dressing

Combine endive, fruit and cereal; toss lightly. Serve with dressing.

6 servings

Confetti Kidney Bean Salad, Sweet 'N Sour Bean Salad (page 62), Ham 'N Rice Salad

Sweet 'N Sour Bean Salad

1/2 cup Kraft oil and
    vinegar dressing
2 tablespoons honey
1 tablespoon mustard
1/2 teaspoon poppy seed
1 16-oz. can cut green beans,
    drained

1 16-oz. can lima beans,
    drained
1 16-oz. can wax beans,
    drained
1/2 cup onion rings
1/4 cup chopped pimiento

Combine dressing, honey, mustard and poppy seed; mix well. Pour over combined remaining ingredients; mix lightly. Chill several hours.

8 servings

Calico Salad

1 1/2 qts. torn lettuce
1 10-oz. pkg. frozen mixed
    vegetables, thawed, drained
1/3 cup Catalina French dressing

1/4 cup chopped onion
2 tablespoons Kraft
    grated parmesan
    cheese

Combine lettuce, vegetables, dressing and onion; toss lightly. Sprinkle with cheese.

4 to 6 servings

El Paso Bean Salad

1 8-oz. bottle Kraft oil and
    vinegar dressing
1 16-oz. can kidney beans,
    drained
1 16-oz. can garbanzo beans,
    drained

1 cup celery slices
1/2 cup chopped onion
1 4-oz. can green chilies,
    chopped
4 crisply cooked bacon
    slices, crumbled

Pour dressing over combined beans, celery, onion and chilies. Cover; marinate in refrigerator several hours or overnight. Drain, reserving marinade. Combine vegetables and bacon; mix lightly. Serve with marinade, if desired.

8 servings

Peachy Cheese Salad

1 1/2 cups cottage cheese
1 8-1/4-oz. can crushed
    pineapple, drained
1/3 cup toasted coconut

1 16-oz. can peach slices,
    drained
Lettuce
Catalina French dressing

Combine cottage cheese and pineapple; mix lightly. Stir in coconut just before serving. Arrange peaches on lettuce-covered plates; top with cottage cheese mixture. Serve with dressing.

4 servings

Autumn Salad

1 1/2 cups shredded carrots
1/3 cup chopped pecans
1/3 cup raisins
    Kraft French dressing
1 16-oz. can pear halves

1/2 cup chopped pitted
    dates
1 3-oz. pkg. Philadelphia
    Brand cream cheese
Lettuce

Combine carrot, nuts, raisins and enough dressing to moisten; mix lightly. Chill. Drain pears, reserving 2 tablespoons syrup. Combine reserved syrup, dates and softened cream cheese, mixing until well blended. Fill each pear half with cream cheese mixture. Spoon carrot mixture onto lettuce-covered platter; top with pears. Garnish pears with pecan halves and serve with additional dressing, if desired.

6 servings

The harvest of colors in this salad makes it an excellent choice for an autumn dinner or buffet.

Mandarin Tossed Salad

1 1/2 qts. torn assorted greens
1 11-oz. can mandarin orange
    segments, drained

1/2 cup French fried onions
Kraft Russian dressing

Combine greens, orange segments and onion; toss lightly. Serve with dressing. Top with additional onion, if desired.

6 to 8 servings

Indiana Macaroni Salad

1 7-1/4-oz. pkg. Kraft macaroni
and cheese dinner
1/4 lb. salami, cut into strips
1/2 cup chopped celery
1/2 cup shredded carrot
1/4 cup finely chopped green
pepper
1/4 cup chopped sweet pickle

2 tablespoons finely
chopped onion
1/2 cup Catalina French
dressing
1/2 cup Miracle Whip salad
dressing

Prepare dinner as directed on package. Add remaining ingredients; mix lightly. Chill. Add additional French dressing before serving, if desired.

4 to 6 servings

Medley Party Salad

1 8-oz. bottle Kraft Italian
dressing
1 16-oz. can cut green beans,
drained
1 16-oz. can sliced carrots,
drained
1 cup celery slices

1 6-oz. can water
chestnuts, drained,
cut in half
1/2 cup pitted ripe olive
slices
2 qts. torn assorted
greens

Pour dressing over combined vegetables. Cover; marinate in refrigerator several hours or overnight. Drain, reserving marinade. Combine vegetables and greens; toss lightly. Serve with marinade.

8 to 10 servings

Buffet Salad Platter

1 10-oz. pkg. frozen Brussels
   sprouts, cooked, drained,
   cut in half
2 cups cauliflowerets,
   partially cooked, drained
1 16-oz. jar sliced beets,
   drained
1 16-oz. jar sliced carrots,
   drained

1 8-oz. bottle Kraft
   Italian dressing
8 ozs. assorted luncheon
   meat slices, folded
1 8-oz. pkg. Kraft aged
   natural Swiss cheese
   slices, cut into
   thirds
Lettuce

Place vegetables in separate containers; pour dressing over vegetables. Cover; marinate in refrigerator several hours or overnight. Drain, reserving marinade. Arrange vegetables, meat and cheese on lettuce-covered platter. Serve with marinade.

6 to 8 servings

Neopolitan Salad

1 16-oz. can tomatoes
1/2 cup Kraft Italian dressing
1 4-oz. can mushrooms, drained
1/2 cup onion rings
1/2 cup pitted ripe olives

1/2 cup garbanzo beans
1 tablespoon dried
   parsley flakes
Lettuce

Drain tomatoes, reserving 1/2 cup liquid. Combine reserved liquid and dressing. Combine 1/2 cup dressing, tomatoes, mushrooms, onion, olives, beans and parsley; mix lightly. Chill. Serve on lettuce-covered plates with remaining dressing, if desired.

4 servings

Variation: Substitute 1 cup fresh tomato wedges for 16-oz. can tomatoes.

Christmas Wreath Salad

1 head romaine
1 16-oz. jar sliced beets,
   drained
1 1/2 cups onion rings
2 4-oz. cans mushrooms,
   drained

1 cup cooked peas,
   chilled
Roka brand blue
   cheese dressing

Line salad bowl with romaine leaves; tear remaining romaine into bite-size pieces. Layer half of romaine, beets, onion, mushrooms and peas. Repeat layers, arranging top layer of vegetables to form wreath. Serve with dressing.

8 servings

Layering canned vegetables of traditional holiday colors creates a festive salad for entertaining.

Hot Spiced Fruit

1 16-oz. can peach halves,
   drained
1 16-oz. can pear halves,
   undrained

1/2 cup Kraft Russian
   dressing
1 teaspoon whole cloves
1 teaspoon cinnamon

Combine ingredients in saucepan. Simmer 15 minutes, stirring occasionally.

4 to 6 servings

A quick and easy compote that makes the perfect meat accompaniment.

Christmas Wreath Salad

Bean 'N Beet Salad

1/2 cup Kraft oil and
   vinegar dressing
1/4 teaspoon dry mustard
1/4 teaspoon rosemary
1 16-oz. can whole green
   beans, drained

1 16-oz. jar crinkle-cut
   beets, drained
Lettuce
1/4 cup (1 oz.) shredded
   Kraft sharp natural
   cheddar cheese

Combine dressing, mustard and rosemary; mix well. Pour over beans and beets. Cover; marinate in refrigerator several hours. Drain, reserving marinade. Serve vegetables on lettuce-covered plates; sprinkle with cheese. Serve with marinade.

4 servings

SALADS

STARTERS, TIDBITS, AND SNACKS

Salads first — a delightful way to introduce the meal. Make them small and simple, just enough to whet the appetite. A colorful arrangement of fresh fruits, a delicate assortment of leafy greens, a slice of melon or a stuffed avocado half served with a flavorful dressing — all are memorable menu "starters."

Instant salads and savory tidbits are also excellent appetizers and snacks. Paired with pourable dressings, various fruit, vegetable and seafood combinations are nutritious ways to nibble. Fresh crudités, such as carrot or celery sticks, mushroom caps, pineapple cubes and apple slices are refreshing dippers for piquant dips. Marinated vegetables, assorted fruit platters and relishes are other favorites. For each serving, allow 1/4 cup to 1/2 cup of salad or relish and four to six crudités.

Marinated Vegetable Tidbits

1 8-oz. bottle Kraft Italian
   dressing
1 pt. cherry tomatoes, cut
   in half
1 16-oz. can small whole
   onions, drained

2 cups zucchini slices
1 10-oz. pkg. frozen
   Brussels sprouts,
   cooked, drained
1 cup pitted ripe olives
1 cup green pepper chunks

Pour dressing over combined vegetables. Cover; marinate in refrigerator overnight, stirring occasionally. Serve with picks.

Antipasto Roma

1 8-oz. Kraft Italian dressing	6 pepperoncini peppers
1/2 lb. pepperoni slices	4 ozs. Casino brand natural brick cheese, cut into sticks
1 cup cherry tomato halves	
1 7-oz. can artichoke hearts, drained, cut in half	1 hard-cooked egg, sliced
1/2 cup pitted ripe olives	1 qt. shredded assorted greens

Pour dressing over pepperoni, tomato, artichoke hearts, olives and peppers. Cover; marinate in refrigerator overnight. Drain, reserving marinade. Arrange pepperoni, vegetables, cheese and egg on lettuce-covered platter. Serve with marinade.

8 to 10 servings

"Antipasto" is Italian for "before the pasta." Traditionally, it is a marvelously arranged platter of marinated vegetables, assorted cheeses and savory meats. It is delicious and festive for casual gatherings or elegant entertaining — indoors or out!

Shrimp Italiano

1 8-oz. bottle Kraft Italian dressing	1 cup pitted ripe olives
2 cups (12 ozs.) cleaned cooked shrimp	

Pour dressing over shrimp and olives. Cover; marinate in refrigerator several hours or overnight. Drain. Serve with picks.

Pinwheel Appetizers

1 3-oz. pkg. Philadelphia Brand cream cheese	1/4 cup chopped onion
1/4 cup Kraft creamy cucumber dressing	1 tablespoon chopped parsley
	1/4 lb. boiled ham slices

Combine softened cream cheese, dressing, onion and parsley, mixing until well blended. Spread ham slices with cream cheese mixture; roll up. Chill. Cut rolls into 1/2-inch slices to serve.

Vegetable Medley

1 8-oz. bottle Kraft Italian
    dressing
1 cup plain yogurt
2 cups cherry tomato halves
2 cups chopped cucumber
1 cup celery slices
1 cup radish slices
1/2 cup green onions, cut
    into 1-inch lengths
Chopped parsley

Combine dressing and yogurt; mix well. Chill. Combine tomato, cucumber, celery, radishes and onion; mix lightly. Chill. Serve with dressing; sprinkle with parsley.

10 to 12 servings

Dover Salad

2 cups torn curly endive
2 cups iceberg lettuce chunks
1 3-3/4-oz. can salmon,
    drained, flaked
1 cup cherry tomato halves
1 cup cucumber slices
Romaine
1 hard-cooked egg yolk,
    sieved
Kraft creamy cucumber
    dressing

Combine greens and salmon; toss lightly. Arrange greens mixture and cucumber on individual romaine-covered plates. Top with egg; serve with dressing.

10 to 12 servings

Curried Party Snack

1/4 cup Kraft oil and vinegar
    dressing
1 teaspoon curry powder
2 cups peanuts
1 1/2 cups bite-size crispy
    wheat squares
1 cup raisins

Combine dressing and curry powder. Pour over combined remaining ingredients; mix lightly. Spread on ungreased 15 1/2 x 10 1/2-inch jelly roll pan. Bake at 350°, 15 minutes, stirring occasionally.

4 1/2 cups

Ensalada Gazpacho

1 cup chopped tomato
1/2 cup Catalina French dressing
1/2 cup chopped cucumber
1/4 cup chopped green pepper
2 tablespoons green onion
   slices

1 teaspoon lime juice
1/2 teaspoon oregano
   leaves, crushed
1/8 teaspoon pepper
4 avocado halves, peeled
1 qt. shredded lettuce

Combine tomato, dressing, cucumber, green pepper, onion, lime juice and seasonings; mix lightly. Place avocados on lettuce-covered plates; fill with vegetable mixture.

4 servings

Marinated Mushrooms

1 8-oz. bottle Kraft Italian
   dressing

1/2 lb. small mushrooms
1/4 cup chopped parsley

Pour dressing over mushrooms and parsley. Cover; marinate in refrigerator several hours or overnight. Drain. Serve with picks.

Party Meatballs

1 lb. ground beef
2 cups soft bread crumbs
1 egg
1/4 cup chopped onion
1 tablespoon chopped parsley
2 tablespoons Parkay margarine

1/2 cup Catalina French
   dressing
1/2 cup Kraft pineapple
   preserves

Combine meat, bread crumbs, egg, onion and parsley; mix lightly. Shape into 1-inch meatballs. Brown in margarine; drain. Place in 2-quart casserole. Combine dressing and preserves; pour over meatballs. Bake at 350°, 30 minutes, stirring occasionally. Serve with picks.

To prevent last minute preparation, prepare the meatballs early in the day and reheat for serving.

Green Onion Dip

3/4 cup Kraft green onion
   dressing

1/2 cup dairy sour cream

Combine ingredients; mix well. Chill. Serve with crackers, potato chips or vegetable dippers.

Approximately 1 cup

Avocado Dip

1 medium avocado, peeled,
   mashed
1/2 cup Kraft green goddess
   dressing

3 crisply cooked bacon
   slices, crumbled

Combine ingredients; mix well. Cover securely; chill. Serve with crisp vegetable dippers or corn chips.

1 1/2 cups

The avocado is sometimes referred to as the "alligator pear" because of the texture of the skin. Avocado halves are attractive containers for fruit and vegetable salads.

Fun Fruit Fondue

1 cup orange segments
1 cup pineapple chunks
1 cup apple wedges
2 bananas, cut into 1-inch
   pieces

Lettuce
3/4 cup Kraft Russian
   dressing
1/2 cup chopped peanuts
1/2 cup shredded coconut

Arrange fruit on lettuce-covered platter. Skewer fruit with picks. Dip in dressing; roll in nuts or coconut.

10 to 12 servings

This year-round fruit fondue is a taste treat for children and adults.

Chunky Blue Cheese Dip

1/2 cup Kraft chunky blue
    cheese dressing
1 8-oz. pkg. Philadelphia
    Brand cream cheese

2 tablespoons finely
    chopped green pepper

Gradually add dressing to softened cream cheese, mixing until well blended. Stir in green pepper. Chill. Serve with vegetable dippers.

1 1/2 cups

Salsa Dip

2 cups finely chopped tomatoes
1 cup finely chopped onion
1/2 cup finely chopped celery
1/4 cup finely chopped green
    pepper

Catalina French dressing
Hot pepper sauce

Combine vegetables and enough dressing to moisten; mix lightly. Season to taste with hot pepper sauce. Chill. Serve with corn chips.

3 1/2 cups

Aloha Party Dip

1 cup dairy sour cream
1/2 cup Kraft chunky blue
    cheese dressing
1 8-1/4-oz. can crushed
    pineapple, drained

1/4 cup slivered almonds,
    toasted
1/2 teaspoon Worcestershire
    sauce
1/4 teaspoon onion powder

Combine sour cream and dressing. Add remaining ingredients; mix well. Chill. Serve with vegetable dippers or crackers.

2 cups

Cocktail Potpourri

Small cooked meatballs
Luncheon meat, cubed
Pineapple chunks, drained
Small whole mushrooms

Catalina French
  dressing
Cleaned cooked shrimp

Combine meatballs, luncheon meat, pineapple, mushrooms and enough dressing to moisten; mix lightly. Simmer 10 minutes, stirring frequently. Add shrimp; continue simmering until hot. Serve in chafing dish with picks.

Holiday Vegetable Dip

1 8-oz. bottle Kraft thousand
  island or creamy Russian
  dressing

1 hard-cooked egg, chopped
2 tablespoons green
  onion slices

Combine dressing, egg and onion; mix well. Chill. Serve with vegetable dippers.

1 cup

Shrimp Appetizers

3 cups (18 ozs.) cleaned
  cooked shrimp
2/3 cup Kraft creamy garlic
  dressing

1/2 cup dry bread crumbs
1/3 cup Kraft grated
  parmesan cheese

Dip shrimp in dressing; coat with combined crumbs and cheese. Place on greased cookie sheet. Bake at 450°, 10 to 15 minutes or until lightly browned.

Cocktail Potpourri, Holiday Vegetable Dip

Chilled Vegetable Spread

1/3 cup Kraft oil and vinegar
    dressing
1 3-oz. pkg. Philadelphia
    Brand cream cheese
1 10-oz. pkg. frozen chopped
    spinach, thawed,
    well-drained

1 cup shredded zucchini
1 cup finely shredded
    carrots
2 tablespoons finely
    chopped onion

Gradually add dressing to softened cream cheese, mixing until well blended. Add combined vegetables; mix well. Spoon mixture into 2-cup mold, lightly brushed with dressing. Chill until firm. Unmold; serve with cucumber slices, crackers or party bread slices.

2 cups

Variation: To make in a blender, place softened cream cheese in blender container. Add dressing; blend until smooth. Add vegetables; blend until well mixed. Continue preparation as directed.

Quick and Easy Snacks

- Serve melon balls, pineapple chunks and apple wedges as dippers with Roka brand blue cheese dressing.
- Marinate artichoke hearts and mushroom caps in Golden caesar dressing for several hours. Drain and serve on picks.
- Serve celery or carrot sticks, broccoli flowerets and cherry tomatoes as dippers with Kraft thousand island or creamy Russian dressing.
- Marinate leftover cooked vegetables in Catalina French dressing and chill.
- Simmer cocktail sausages or ham cubes in Kraft Russian dressing. Keep warm in chafing dish or over warmer.

SALADS

MAIN EVENTS

In America, salads have gained such prominence that they are frequently the featured attraction at family and party meals. Main dish or entrée salads are particulary appealing during the summer season when cool meals are a refreshing relief on hot, lazy days. There are also hot and hearty favorites to warm up winter menus. Cold or hot, entrée salads are especially popular with the family cook since they are easy to prepare, can be made in advance and can be complete one-dish meals.

To rank as a main dish, a salad should provide one or more protein foods such as meat, poultry, fish, eggs, cheese or nuts. An easy guide to ingredient selection is the basic food groups. Choosing at least one ingredient from each of the groups is the beginning of an attractive, nourishing salad since the groups automatically provide variety in color, flavor, texture, shapes and nutritive value.

Lorraine Salad

6 hard-cooked eggs, chopped
4 crisply cooked bacon slices, crumbled
1/2 cup (2 ozs.) shredded Kraft natural Swiss cheese
1/2 cup celery slices
1/2 cup Kraft coleslaw dressing
1/4 cup green onion slices
Patty shells or toast cups

Combine eggs, bacon, cheese, celery, dressing and onion; mix lightly. Chill. Spoon egg mixture into patty shells or toast cups.

4 to 6 servings

This main course salad combines the tasty ingredients of quiche lorraine in a chilled luncheon salad.

Club Egg Salad

1 1/2 cups iceberg lettuce chunks
6 hard-cooked eggs, sliced
3/4 cup shredded carrot
1/2 cup chopped green pepper
1/4 cup green onion slices
2 tablespoons chopped parsley

Dash of pepper
4 crisply cooked bacon
    slices, crumbled
1 cup tomato wedges
    Miracle French dressing

Combine lettuce, eggs, carrot, green pepper, onion, parsley and pepper; toss lightly. Sprinkle with bacon; garnish with tomato. Serve with dressing.

4 servings

Cottage Cheese Luncheon Salad

3 cups cottage cheese
1 cup radish slices
1 tablespoon chopped chives
1 teaspoon salt
    Dash of pepper

Lettuce
2 tomatoes, sliced
3/4 cup cucumber slices
    Kraft garlic French
    dressing

Combine cottage cheese, radishes, chives and seasonings; mix lightly. For each serving, place cottage cheese mixture on lettuce-covered plate; surround with tomato and cucumber. Serve with dressing.

6 servings

Hot Chicken Salad

3 cups chopped cooked chicken
1 cup celery slices
1/2 cup Kraft coleslaw dressing
1/4 cup green onion slices
2 tablespoons chopped pimiento
1 teaspoon salt

1/8 teaspoon pepper
1 cup (4 ozs.) shredded
    Kraft natural Swiss
    cheese
1 tablespoon flour

Combine chicken, celery, dressing, onion, pimiento and seasonings; mix well. Toss cheese with flour. Add to chicken mixture; mix lightly. Spoon into 1-quart casserole. Bake at 350°, 30 minutes.

4 to 6 servings

Golden Pasta Salad

1 8-oz. bottle Kraft golden
    blend Italian dressing
2 cups cherry tomato halves
1 cup zucchini slices
1/2 cup pitted ripe olive slices
1/4 lb. salami, cut into strips
1/2 cup Kraft real mayonnaise

2 tablespoons Kraft
    grated parmesan cheese
2 tablespoons green
    onion slices
7 ozs. spaghetti, cooked,
    drained, chilled

Pour dressing over tomato, zucchini, olives and meat. Cover; marinate in your refrigerator several hours or overnight. Drain, reserving 1/2 cup marinade. Combine marinade, mayonnaise, cheese and onion; mix well. Combine 1/4 cup mayonnaise mixture with spaghetti; toss lightly. Top spaghetti with vegetable mixture and remaining mayonnaise mixture.

4 servings

Pasta takes a new twist when tossed with marinated meat, vegetables and cheese. Serve with bread sticks and wine for a true Italian meal.

Cobb Salad Platter

1 8-oz. bottle Kraft French
    dressing
1/2 cup (2 ozs.) crumbled Kraft
    cold pack blue cheese
4 crisply cooked bacon slices,
    crumbled
2 cups chopped tomatoes

2 cups chopped cooked
    chicken
2 hard-cooked eggs,
    chopped
1 avocado, peeled,
    chopped
1 1/2 qts. shredded lettuce

Combine dressing, cheese and bacon; mix well. Chill. Arrange tomato, chicken, eggs and avocado on lettuce-covered platter. Garnish with additional bacon, if desired. Serve with dressing.

6 servings

Variation: Add green pepper chunks, celery slices or croutons.

This recipe was inspired by the salad developed by the Brown Derby restaurant in Los Angeles.

Golden Pasta Salad, Cobb Salad Platter

Lunchtime Salad Bowl

1 1/2 qts. torn assorted greens
1 cup luncheon meat strips
1/4 cup dill pickle slices
2 hard-cooked eggs, chopped
2 tablespoons chopped onion

Kraft thousand island
or creamy Russian
dressing

Combine greens, meat, pickle, eggs and onion; toss lightly.
Serve with dressing.

4 servings

Beef 'N Cheddar Salad

3/4 cup Kraft creamy cucumber
dressing
3 tablespoons Kraft
horseradish sauce
1 tablespoon chopped parsley
2 cups shredded lettuce
1 cup torn romaine
1 cup torn curly endive

2 cups shredded red
cabbage
1/2 lb. roast beef slices
1 1/2 cups tomato slices
4 ozs. Kraft sharp
natural cheddar cheese,
cut into strips
1 cup onion rings

Combine dressing, horseradish sauce and parsley; mix well.
Combine greens and cabbage; toss lightly. Place greens mixture
on platter; arrange remaining ingredients on greens. Serve with
dressing.

4 to 6 servings

Bouquet Salad

1 8-oz. bottle Kraft Italian
or golden blend Italian
dressing
1/4 cup dry white wine
2 cups (6 ozs.) bow noodles,
cooked, drained
2 cups broccoli flowerets

2 cups chopped cooked
chicken
2 cups mushroom halves
3/4 cup red pepper chunks
1/2 cup onion rings
2 tablespoons Kraft grated
parmesan cheese

Combine dressing and wine; pour over combined noodles,
broccoli, chicken, mushrooms, red peppers and onion. Cover;
marinate in refrigerator several hours. Sprinkle with cheese just
before serving.

4 servings

Hearty Potato Salad

1 qt. cooked potato slices
2 cups roast beef strips
1 cup mushroom slices
1 cup red onion rings
1/4 cup chopped parsley

3/4 cup Kraft creamy garlic
  dressing
1/2 cup Kraft real
  mayonnaise
1/4 teaspoon pepper

Combine potatoes, meat, mushrooms, onion and parsley. Add combined garlic dressing, mayonnaise and pepper; mix lightly. Chill. Add additional garlic dressing before serving, if desired.

4 to 6 servings

Curry Ham Salad

2 cups chopped ham or cooked
  turkey
1 8-1/4-oz. can pineapple
  chunks, drained
1 cup celery slices
1 cup grape halves

1/2 cup peanuts
1/8 teaspoon curry powder
  Kraft thousand island
  or creamy Russian
  dressing

Combine ham, pineapple, celery, grapes, nuts, curry powder and enough dressing to moisten; mix lightly. Chill. Serve on lettuce with additional dressing, if desired.

4 servings

Chef's Salad

1 1/2 qts. torn assorted greens
1/2 cup cucumber slices
1 cup tomato wedges
4 hard-cooked eggs, sliced
4 ozs. cooked beef tongue, cut
  into julienne strips
1/2 cup cooked chicken, cut
  into julienne strips

2 ozs. Kraft natural
  Swiss cheese, cut into
  julienne strips
Kraft thousand island
  or creamy Russian
  dressing

Combine greens and cucumber; toss lightly. Arrange tomato, eggs, meat, chicken and cheese on greens. Serve with dressing.

4 servings

Alpine Potato Salad

1 1/2 qts. quartered cooked new
    potatoes
2 cups shredded red cabbage
2 cups ham strips
1 cup celery slices
1/4 cup green onion slices
3/4 cup Kraft Italian dressing

1 tablespoon Kraft pure
    prepared mustard
8 ozs. Kraft natural
    Swiss cheese, cut
    into strips

Combine potatoes, cabbage, meat, celery and onion. Add combined dressing and mustard; mix lightly. Chill. Add cheese just before serving; mix lightly.

8 to 10 servings

Deluxe Luncheon Salad

1 qt. torn lettuce
2 cups broccoli flowerets
1 cup roast beef strips
1 cup mushroom slices

1 cup red onion rings
Kraft chunky blue
    cheese dressing

Combine lettuce, broccoli, meat, mushrooms and onion; toss lightly. Serve with dressing.

4 servings

Tropical Tuna Salad

2 cups pineapple chunks
1 cup tomato slices
1 6-1/2-oz. can tuna,
    drained, flaked
1/2 cup celery slices
1/4 cup pitted ripe olive wedges

2 tablespoons chopped
    parsley
Lettuce cups
Kraft creamy cucumber
    dressing

Combine pineapple, tomato, tuna, celery, olives and parsley; mix lightly. Spoon into lettuce cups; serve with dressing.

4 servings

Alpine Potato Salad

Layered Chicken Salad

1 cup dairy sour cream
3/4 cup Kraft thousand island
   or creamy Russian dressing
2 tablespoons Kraft blue
   cheese crumbles
2 cups chopped cooked chicken
1/2 teaspoon salt
1/8 teaspoon pepper

1 qt. shredded lettuce
2 cups carrot slices
1 cup zucchini slices
1 cup red or green pepper
   rings
1 10-oz. pkg. frozen
   peas, thawed,
   drained

Combine sour cream, dressing and cheese; mix well. Chill. Combine chicken and seasonings; mix lightly. In 2 1/2-quart bowl, layer lettuce, carrot, zucchini, chicken, red pepper and peas. Chill. Serve with dressing.

6 to 8 servings

Shrimp Salad

1 cup cleaned cooked shrimp
3 hard-cooked eggs, chopped
1/2 cup shredded carrot
2 tablespoons green onion
   slices
1/4 teaspoon salt
1/8 teaspoon pepper

Kraft green goddess
   dressing
Lettuce
12 tomato slices
1/4 cup pitted ripe olive
   wedges

Combine shrimp, eggs, carrot, onion, seasonings and enough dressing to moisten; mix lightly. Chill. Spoon shrimp mixture onto lettuce-covered platter; surround with tomato and olives.

4 servings

Sundae Tuna Salad

2 6-1/2-oz. cans tuna,
   drained, flaked
2 hard-cooked eggs, chopped
1/2 cup chopped celery
1/4 cup chopped green pepper

1/3 cup Kraft creamy
   cucumber dressing
6 lettuce slices
1 cup tomato wedges

Combine tuna, eggs, celery, green pepper and dressing; mix lightly. Chill. For each serving, scoop tuna mixture onto lettuce slice; garnish with tomato. Serve with additional dressing, if desired.

4 servings

Chicken Divan Salad

1 8-oz. bottle Kraft French
    dressing
1/4 teaspoon tarragon, crushed
3 cups chopped cooked chicken
1 cup (4 ozs.) shredded
    Kraft natural Swiss
    cheese

1 cup broccoli flowerets
1 cup broccoli stalk slices
1/2 cup sliced almonds,
    toasted
1/2 teaspoon salt
Lettuce

Combine dressing and tarragon; mix well. Combine chicken, cheese, broccoli, nuts and salt; mix lightly. Serve on lettuce-covered plates. Garnish with additional nuts, if desired. Serve with dressing.

6 servings

Russian Potato Salad

1/2 cup chopped onion
1/2 cup chopped green pepper
1 8-oz. bottle Kraft Russian
    dressing

6 cups chopped cooked
    potatoes
1 lb. ham, cut into strips
Salt and pepper

Sauté onion and green pepper in dressing over low heat. Add potatoes and ham; toss lightly. Season to taste. Heat, stirring occasionally.

6 to 8 servings

Variation: Substitute Kraft creamy Russian or thousand island dressing for Russian dressing.

Coastline Salad Bowl

1 qt. torn assorted greens
1 6-1/2-oz. can tuna, drained,
    flaked
1/2 cup radish slices
1/2 cup cucumber slices, halved

2 hard-cooked eggs
Kraft thousand island
    or creamy Russian
    dressing

Combine greens, tuna, radishes, cucumber and chopped egg whites; toss lightly. Top with sieved egg yolks; serve with dressing.

4 servings

Seaside Cucumber Salad

1 15-1/2-oz. can salmon
   drained, flaked
1 cup chopped cucumber
1/4 cup onion rings
2 tablespoons chopped parsley

6 avocado halves, peeled
Lettuce
Kraft creamy cucumber
   dressing

Combine salmon, cucumber, onion and parsley; mix lightly. Place avocados on lettuce-covered platter; fill with salmon mixture. Serve with dressing.

6 servings

Variation: Substitute two 6 1/2-oz. cans tuna, drained, flaked, for salmon.

A sophisticated salmon salad attractively served in avocado halves. A refreshing luncheon or supper salad.

Polynesian Shrimp Salad

1/2 cup Kraft chunky blue
   cheese dressing
1/2 cup dairy sour cream
2 pineapples
2 cups (10 ozs.) cleaned
   cooked shrimp

1 1/2 cups grape halves
1 cup melon balls
1/3 cup green onion slices

Combine dressing and sour cream; mix well. Chill. Cut pineapples in half lengthwise through crown. Remove fruit, leaving shells intact. Core fruit; cut into chunks. Combine with shrimp, grapes, melon and onion; mix lightly. Spoon into pineapple shells; top with dressing.

4 servings

Variation: Substitute 2 cups chopped cooked chicken for shrimp.

Frozen, fresh or canned shrimp are suitable for this recipe. For melon balls, use cantaloupe, honeydew, casaba or Persian melon.

SALADS

SALADS WITH A SHAPE

Simple or elegant, tall or small, clear or creamy, molded salads add style to almost any dining occasion. Another attribute is their complete do-ahead preparation which is a welcome convenience for balancing busy schedules and for entertaining.

When selecting a recipe, consider the occasion. For example, tall sophisticated molds add special interest to party buffets. Dainty individual molds highlight luncheon salad plates. Salads made in covered baking pans are excellent portable fare for picnics or potluck suppers. Salads molded in attractive glass bowls can be served right from the bowl without unmolding.

Most molded salads are made with gelatin. There are, however, some salad mixtures such as rice, macaroni and potato salads which will hold their shape when simply pressed into a mold and chilled. For either type, pourable dressings add flavor and stability. French, coleslaw, creamy cucumber, blue cheese and thousand island are just a few of the many dressing choices which enhance molded salads.

The Shape of Success

Appearance is an important consideration for gelatin salads; therefore, a few preparation precautions are the best guidelines to success.

- Brush molds lightly with oil when preparing gelatin salads. Remove excess with a paper towel.
- Add liquid ingredients gradually to salad dressing or mayonnaise, never the reverse. Stir constantly until well blended.

- Chill gelatin mixtures until the consistency resembles thick, unbeaten egg whites when the recipe states: "Chill until partially set."
- Chill each layer of a two- or three-layered mold until firm yet sticky to the touch before adding successive layers.
- Chill six to eight hours or overnight before serving.
- Loosen the edge of a gelatin mold by carefully running the tip of a knife or metal spatula around the rim.
- Dip the mold container into warm water, just to the upper rim, or cover with a warm wet cloth. Shake the mold gently to loosen the gelatin.
- Unmold gelatin salad onto a moistened plate so it can be easily repositioned, if necessary.

Limelight Pineapple Mold

1 3-oz. pkg. lime flavored
 gelatin
1 3-oz. pkg. lemon flavored
 gelatin
2 cups boiling water
1 20-oz. can crushed pineapple
1 8-oz. bottle Kraft coleslaw
 dressing
1 8-oz. pkg. Philadelphia
 Brand cream cheese
Cold water
1/2 cup chopped nuts
Lettuce
4 cups cantaloupe balls

Dissolve gelatin in boiling water; cool. Drain pineapple, reserving syrup. Combine 1/4 cup reserved syrup, dressing and softened cream cheese, mixing until well blended. Add enough cold water to remaining reserved syrup to measure 1 cup; add to gelatin. Add 1 cup dressing mixture to gelatin mixture, mixing until blended. Chill until partially set; fold in pineapple and nuts. Pour into lightly oiled 6-cup ring mold; chill until firm. Unmold; surround with lettuce. Fill center with melon; serve with dressing mixture.

6 to 8 servings

Snappy Salmon Mold

2 envelopes unflavored gelatin
1 1/2 cups cold water
1 cup Miracle Whip salad
  dressing
1/2 cup Kraft French dressing
1/2 cup dairy sour cream
1 1-lb. can salmon,
  drained, flaked
1 cup chopped celery

Soften gelatin in cold water; stir over low heat until dissolved. Cool. Gradually add gelatin to salad dressing, French dressing and sour cream, mixing until blended. Chill until partially set; fold in salmon and celery. Pour into lightly oiled 1 1/2-quart mold; chill until firm. Unmold; garnish with curly endive, if desired.

6 servings

This savory salmon mold is an excellent entrée salad, especially for luncheons. For a buffet attraction, serve the mold on a large platter surrounded by a variety of fresh vegetables such as cucumber twists, tomato wedges, carrot curls and radish roses.

Creamy Cucumber Mold

2 envelopes unflavored
  gelatin
1 cup cold water
2/3 cup Kraft creamy cucumber
  dressing
1/4 teaspoon salt
1/8 teaspoon pepper
1 1/2 cups shredded cucumber,
  drained
1 cup heavy cream,
  whipped
1 tablespoon finely
  chopped onion

Soften gelatin in cold water; stir over low heat until dissolved. Cool. Gradually add gelatin to combined dressing, salt and pepper, mixing until blended. Chill until partially set; fold in cucumber, whipped cream and onion. Pour into lightly oiled 5-cup mold; chill until firm. Unmold; garnish with cucumber slices, if desired.

8 to 10 servings

Snappy Salmon Mold, Creamy Cucumber Mold

Marinated Vegetable Ring

1/2 cup Miracle French dressing
1 16-oz. can cut green beans, drained
1/2 cup carrot slices
1/2 cup celery slices
1/2 cup pitted ripe olives

* * *

2 envelopes unflavored gelatin

1 1/2 cups cold water
2 cups cottage cheese
1 cup Miracle Whip salad dressing
1 cup milk
1/2 cup chopped parsley
1/4 cup chopped onion

Pour dressing over combined beans, carrot, celery and olives. Cover; marinate in refrigerator several hours or overnight. Drain.

Soften gelatin in 1 cup cold water; stir over low heat until dissolved. Add remaining water. Gradually add gelatin to combined cottage cheese, salad dressing and milk, mixing until blended. Chill until partially set; fold in parsley and onion. Pour into lightly oiled 6-cup ring mold; chill until firm. Unmold; fill center with marinated vegetables.

8 servings

Pastel Fruit Mold

3 envelopes unflavored gelatin
1 1/2 cups cold water
2 cups lemon-lime soda
1 cup pear slices
1/2 cup peach slices
1/2 cup plum slices
1 8-oz. bottle Kraft French dressing

1/4 cup honey
1/4 teaspoon coriander
1/2 cup heavy cream, whipped
Lettuce

Soften gelatin in cold water; stir over low heat until dissolved. Gradually add soda. Pour 1 cup gelatin mixture into lightly oiled 9-inch layer pan. Arrange pear, peach and plum slices in gelatin. Chill until almost set. Combine remaining gelatin mixture, dressing, honey and coriander; fold in whipped cream. Pour over molded layer; chill until firm. Unmold; surround with lettuce.

8 servings

Piquant Cucumber Mold

1 3-oz. pkg. lime flavored
gelatin
1/2 teaspoon salt
1 cup boiling water
1/2 cup Kraft creamy cucumber
dressing

1/4 cup dairy sour cream
1 tablespoon Kraft
prepared horseradish
1 1/2 cups chopped cucumber
1 tablespoon grated onion

Dissolve gelatin and salt in boiling water; cool. Gradually add gelatin to combined dressing, sour cream and horseradish, mixing until blended. Chill until partially set; fold in cucumber and onion. Pour into lightly oiled 1-quart mold; chill until firm. Unmold; garnish with tomato wedges and curly endive, if desired.

4 to 6 servings

Blue Cheese Ring

2 envelopes unflavored gelatin
1 cup cold water
1 8-oz. bottle Kraft chunky
blue cheese dressing
1 cup heavy cream, whipped

Lettuce
1/2 cup chopped apples
1/2 cup grapes
1/2 cup orange sections

Soften gelatin in cold water; stir over low heat until dissolved. Cool. Gradually add gelatin to dressing, mixing until blended. Chill until partially set; fold in whipped cream. Pour into lightly oiled 1-quart mold; chill until firm. Unmold; surround with lettuce. Serve with combined fruit.

4 to 6 servings

Mandarin Cantaloupe Salad

1/2 cup heavy cream, whipped
1/4 cup Catalina French dressing
1 3-oz. pkg. orange flavored
gelatin
1 cup boiling water

3/4 cup cold water
1 11-oz. can mandarin
orange segments,
drained
2 cantaloupes, halved

Fold whipped cream into dressing. Chill. Dissolve gelatin in boiling water. Add cold water. Chill until partially set; fold in orange segments. Pour mixture into melon halves; chill until firm. Cut melon halves into thirds; serve with dressing.

12 servings

Guacamole Ring

1 envelope unflavored gelatin
1 cup cold water
1/2 cup Kraft Italian dressing
1 1/2 cups mashed avocado
1/2 cup dairy sour cream

1 tablespoon finely
  chopped onion
Dash of hot pepper
  sauce
Mexi Bean Salad

Soften gelatin in 1/4 cup cold water; stir over low heat until dissolved. Add remaining water and dressing. Gradually add gelatin mixture to combined avocado, sour cream, onion and hot pepper sauce, mixing until blended. Pour into 3 1/2-cup ring mold; chill until firm. Unmold just before serving; fill center with:

Mexi Bean Salad

1 16-oz. can kidney beans,
  drained
1/2 cup celery slices
1/4 cup chopped sweet pickle

1/4 cup Kraft French
  dressing

Combine ingredients; mix lightly. Chill several hours or overnight.

6 to 8 servings

Liver Sausage Mold

1 envelope unflavored gelatin
1/2 cup cold water
1 8-oz. bottle Kraft creamy
  Italian dressing

1/2 lb. liver sausage
1/2 cup finely chopped
  green pepper
Curly endive

Soften gelatin in cold water; stir over low heat until dissolved. Cool. Gradually add gelatin to combined dressing, liver sausage and green pepper, mixing until blended. Pour into lightly oiled 3-cup mold; chill until firm. Unmold; surround with curly endive. Serve with party rye bread slices.

3 cups

A flavorful molded spread seasoned with Italian dressing can be made in advance — easy and appetizing for your next party.

Avocado Aspic

2 envelopes unflavored gelatin
1 cup cold water
1 1/2 cups tomato juice
1/2 cup Kraft French dressing
1 tablespoon lemon juice
1/8 teaspoon hot pepper sauce
2 avocados, peeled
1/2 cup finely chopped celery
1/4 cup finely chopped green pepper
1/4 cup finely chopped onion
Lettuce
Shrimp

Soften gelatin in cold water; stir over low heat until dissolved. Gradually add gelatin to combined tomato juice, dressing, lemon juice and hot pepper sauce, mixing until blended. Chill until partially set. Chop one avocado; fold chopped avocado, celery, green pepper and onion into gelatin mixture. Pour into lightly oiled 1-quart mold; chill until firm. Unmold; surround with lettuce. Serve with shrimp and second avocado, sliced.

6 servings.

This decorative avocado salad adds a festive touch to Mexican meals. Garnish with a swirl of mayonnaise, if desired.

Autumn Berry Salad

1/2 cup Kraft Russian dressing
2 tablespoons orange juice
1/4 teaspoon grated orange rind
1/2 cup heavy cream, whipped
2 3-oz. pkgs. orange flavored gelatin
3 cups boiling water
1 16-oz. can whole berry cranberry sauce
1 11-oz. can mandarin orange segments, drained

Combine dressing, orange juice and rind; mix well. Fold in whipped cream. Chill. Dissolve gelatin in boiling water. Chill until partially set; fold in cranberry sauce and orange segments. Pour into lightly oiled 6-cup ring mold. Chill until firm; unmold. Serve with dressing.

8 to 10 servings

Molded Slaw

1 3-oz. pkg. lemon flavored
  gelatin
1/2 teaspoon salt
1 cup boiling water
3/4 cup Kraft coleslaw dressing
2 cups shredded cabbage

1/2 cup shredded carrot
2 tablespoons chopped
  red pepper
1 tablespoon finely
  chopped onion
Lettuce

Dissolve gelatin and salt in boiling water; cool. Gradually add dressing, mixing until blended. Chill until partially set; fold in cabbage, carrot, red pepper and onion. Pour into lightly oiled 1-quart mold; chill until firm. Unmold; surround with lettuce. Garnish with red pepper rings, if desired.

4 to 6 servings

Potato Salad Ring

1 qt. chopped cooked potatoes
1/4 cup green onion slices
4 crisply cooked bacon slices,
  crumbled
1/8 teaspoon pepper
1/2 cup Kraft thousand island
  or creamy Russian dressing

Lettuce
2 cups cherry tomato halves
1 cup green pepper strips
1 cup celery slices

Combine potatoes, onion, bacon and pepper. Add dressing; mix lightly. Press into lightly oiled 6-cup ring mold; chill. Unmold; surround with lettuce. Fill center with combined tomato, green pepper and celery. Serve with additional dressing, if desired.

6 servings

A simple potato salad gains added appeal when molded in a ring or 1 1/2-quart mixing bowl and served with colorful fresh vegetables.

SALADS
FOREIGN INTRIGUE

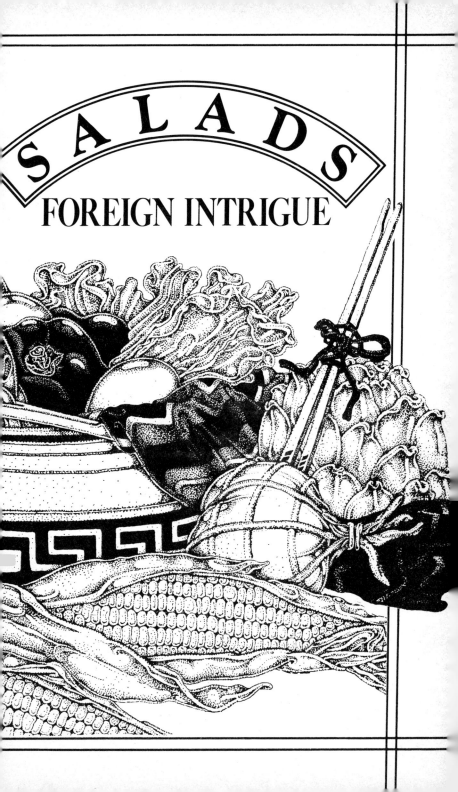

American salads are renowned throughout the world for their tremendous variety and style. Much of this variety is owed to the marvelous year-round abundance of fresh produce which provides great latitude for culinary creativity. Yet, an equally important consideration is our international heritage. Many salads that are now accepted as traditional favorites have been adapted from salads or foods originally introduced by early settlers who immigrated to the New World from many countries.

In recent years, international tourism has expanded our salad horizons as enthusiastic travelers have returned from abroad with new knowledge of foreign cuisines. Such intriguing salads as Antipasto Napoli, Salad Niçoise and Taxco Salad have been adapted for you by the Kraft Kitchens.

Shanghai Seafood Salad

1 8-oz. bottle Kraft oil and
   vinegar dressing
1 tablespoon soy sauce
1/4 teaspoon ginger
2 cups (10 ozs.) cleaned
   cooked shrimp

2 cups celery slices
1 cup (8 ozs.) cooked
   scallops
1/4 cup chopped parsley
2 cups cooked rice,
   chilled

Combine dressing, soy sauce and ginger; mix well. Pour over combined shrimp, celery, scallops and parsley. Cover; marinate in refrigerator overnight. Drain, reserving marinade. Arrange shrimp mixture on rice. Serve with marinade.

6 servings

Variation: Substitute .2-oz. pkg. cellophane noodles for rice. Heat 1/2 cup oil to 375° in heavy skillet. Fry noodles, stirring once. Drain on absorbent paper.

Napoli Bread Salad

1 8-oz. bottle Kraft Italian
   dressing
1 cup cherry tomato halves
1 cup zucchini slices
1 cup mushrooms
1 cup celery slices

1/4 cup chopped parsley
1 qt. Italian bread cubes
1/4 cup (1 oz.) Kraft
   grated parmesan cheese
Romaine

Pour dressing over tomato, zucchini, mushrooms, celery and parsley. Cover; marinate in refrigerator several hours or overnight. Drain, reserving marinade. Combine vegetables, 1/2 cup marinade, bread and cheese; mix lightly. Arrange on romaine-covered platter. Serve with marinade, if desired.

8 to 10 servings

Green Bean Vinaigrette

1 lb. green beans, cooked
1 cup chopped tomato
1/4 cup chopped onion
1/4 cup chopped parsley
1 tablespoon capers

1/2 cup Kraft oil and
   vinegar dressing
Lettuce
1 hard-cooked egg, sieved

Combine beans, tomato, onion, parsley, capers and dressing; mix lightly. Chill several hours. Serve on lettuce-covered platter; sprinkle with egg.

4 to 6 servings

Variation: Substitute 16-oz. can cut green beans for fresh.

Polynesian Fruit Salad

1 pineapple
2 kiwi fruit, peeled, sliced
1 cup papaya balls
1/4 cup almonds, toasted

1 teaspoon shredded
   ginger root
Catalina French
   dressing

Cut pineapple in half lengthwise through crown. Remove fruit, leaving shells intact. Core fruit; cut into chunks. Combine with kiwi, papaya, nuts and ginger root; mix lightly. Spoon fruit mixture into pineapple shells; serve with dressing.

4 servings

Antipasto Napoli

1 cup Kraft Italian dressing
2 cups tomato wedges
2 cups mushroom slices
1/2 lb. summer sausage, cut
    into strips
1 cup zucchini slices

1 7-oz. can artichoke
    hearts, drained,
    quartered
2 qts. torn assorted
    greens

Pour dressing over tomato, mushrooms, sausage, zucchini and artichoke hearts. Cover; marinate in refrigerator several hours. Drain, reserving marinade. Combine vegetables, sausage and greens; toss lightly. Sprinkle with grated parmesan cheese, if desired. Serve with marinade.

4 to 6 servings

Strata Salad Italienne

2 9-oz. pkgs. frozen Italian
    green beans, thawed,
    drained
1 8-oz. bottle Kraft Italian
    dressing
2 cups (4 ozs.) mostaccioli,
    cooked, drained

1 tablespoon chopped parsley
2 cups roast beef strips
2 cups chopped tomato
1 cup red onion rings
6 ozs. Kraft natural
    provolone cheese slices,
    cut into strips

Sauté beans in 1/3 cup dressing until crisp-tender. Combine mostaccioli and parsley. In glass salad bowl, layer mostaccioli mixture, meat, beans, tomato and onion. Pour remaining dressing over salad. Cover; chill several hours or overnight. Top with cheese just before serving. Garnish with tomato wedges and parsley, if desired.

8 to 10 servings

Mango Fruit Salad

2 mangoes, sliced
2 bananas, sliced
2 cups honeydew melon balls
1 cup strawberry halves

1/2 cup fresh shredded
    coconut
Kraft Russian dressing

Combine fruit and coconut; mix lightly. Serve with dressing.

8 servings

Salad Firenze

1 8-oz. bottle Kraft Italian
    dressing
2 cups mushroom slices
1 cup broccoli flowerets
1 cup red onion rings
1/4 lb. salami or summer
    sausage, cubed

2 qts. torn assorted
    greens
1 6-oz. pkg. Kraft
    natural low moisture
    part-skim mozzarella
    cheese slices, cut
    into strips

Pour dressing over vegetables and sausage. Cover; marinate in refrigerator several hours. Drain, reserving marinade. Combine greens and enough marinade to moisten; toss lightly. Add vegetables, sausage and cheese; toss lightly.

4 servings

Oriental Vegetable Salad

1 cup Kraft oil and vinegar
    dressing
2 tablespoons soy sauce
2 teaspoons sesame seed
2 qts. torn bok choy leaves
    or spinach

1 qt. torn nappa or lettuce
1 cup sliced bok choy
    stalks or celery
1 cup bean sprouts
1 cup carrot sticks
1/2 cup radish slices

Combine dressing, soy sauce and sesame seed; mix well. Combine remaining ingredients; toss lightly. Serve with dressing.

10 servings

Bok choy or Chinese chard is an inexpensive green and a popular oriental vegetable.

Danish Salad

1 8-oz. bottle Kraft red wine
    vinegar and oil dressing
1/2 teaspoon dill weed
1 1/2 qts. torn spinach
4 hard-cooked eggs, sliced

1 cup cherry tomato halves
1/2 cup chopped cucumber
1/2 cup red onion rings
1 3-3/4-oz. can sardines,
    drained

Combine dressing and dill weed; mix well. Combine remaining ingredients; toss lightly. Serve with dressing.

6 servings

Iceberg Estrellita Salad

1 cup chopped tomato
1 cup green pepper strips
1 cup chopped cucumber
1/4 cup Catalina French dressing
1 head iceberg lettuce, cut
    into 6 wedges
1 cup corn chips
1/4 cup (2 ozs.) shredded
    Kraft sharp natural
    cheddar cheese

Combine tomato, green pepper, cucumber and dressing; mix lightly. Chill. Arrange lettuce in pinwheel fashion on serving platter. Combine vegetable mixture and corn chips; mix lightly. Spoon over lettuce; top with cheese. Serve with additional dressing, if desired.

6 servings

Taxco Salad

1 1/2 lbs. ground beef
1 16-oz. can kidney beans,
    drained
1 8-oz. bottle Catalina
    French dressing
1 tablespoon chili powder
1/2 teaspoon salt
2 1/2 cups chopped tomatoes
1 cup chopped green pepper

*   *   *

2 avocados, peeled, mashed

1/2 cup Miracle Whip
    salad dressing
1/4 cup chopped onion
4 crisply cooked bacon
    slices, crumbled
1/2 teaspoon salt
    Dash of hot pepper
    sauce
    Tortilla chips
3 cups shredded lettuce

Brown meat; drain. Stir in beans, 2/3 cup dressing and seasonings. Cover; simmer 10 minutes over low heat, stirring occasionally. Combine tomato, green pepper and 1/3 cup dressing; mix lightly.

Combine avocado, salad dressing, onion, bacon and seasonings; mix well. For each salad, top tortilla chips with lettuce, tomato mixture, meat mixture and avocado mixture. Garnish with chili peppers, if desired.

4 to 6 servings

This recipe, which blends popular Mexican flavors, has long been a Kraft Kitchens favorite.

Iceberg Estrellita Salad, Taxco Salad

Tokyo Vegetable Toss

1 8-oz. bottle Kraft Italian
    dressing
1 lb. green beans, cooked,
    drained
2 cups broccoli flowerets
1 1/2 cups mushroom slices

1 cup bean sprouts
8 ozs. tofu, well-drained,
    cut into 1-inch cubes
Lettuce
1/4 cup French fried onions

Pour 3/4 cup dressing over beans, broccoli, mushrooms and bean sprouts. Cover; marinate in refrigerator several hours or overnight. Pour remaining dressing over tofu. Cover; marinate in refrigerator 2 hours. Drain vegetables and tofu, reserving marinade. Arrange vegetables and tofu on lettuce-covered platter; sprinkle with onions. Serve with marinade, if desired.

8 servings

Lettuce Crêpes

1 8-oz. pkg. Philadelphia
    Brand cream cheese
2 tablespoons Kraft thousand
    island or creamy Russian
    dressing
1 8-1/4-oz. can crushed
    pineapple, well-drained

1/2 cup finely chopped ham
1/4 cup chopped green
    pepper
6 leaf lettuce leaves

Combine softened cream cheese and dressing, mixing until well blended. Add pineapple, ham and green pepper; mix well. Spread mixture on lettuce; roll up. Secure with picks; chill until firm. Remove picks. Serve with additional dressing, if desired.

6 servings

Borscht Salad

1 qt. shredded red cabbage
2 cups cooked potato slices
1 16-oz. jar julienne beets,
    drained
1/2 cup chopped green pepper

1/2 cup Kraft red wine
    vinegar and oil
    dressing
1/2 teaspoon salt
1 cup dairy sour cream

Combine cabbage, potatoes, beets, green pepper, dressing and salt; mix lightly. Chill. Blend in sour cream just before serving.

8 servings

Mount Olympus Salad

1 8-oz. bottle Golden caesar
   dressing
2 cups cucumber slices
1 cup onion rings
1 cup green pepper strips
1 6-oz. can pitted ripe
   olives, drained

1 2-oz. can rolled
   anchovy fillets
1/4 cup (2 ozs.) crumbled
   feta cheese
1 qt. shredded lettuce

Pour dressing over cucumber, onion, green pepper and olives. Cover; marinate in refrigerator several hours. Drain, reserving marinade. Arrange vegetables, anchovy fillets and cheese on lettuce-covered platter. Garnish with lemon wedges, if desired. Serve with marinade.

4 to 6 servings

Salade Aux Endives

Belgian endive
Artichoke hearts, cut
   in half
Radish slices

Bibb lettuce
Kraft oil and vinegar
   dressing

Arrange vegetables on lettuce-covered plates. Serve with dressing.

Mali Fruit Salad

1/4 cup Kraft Russian dressing
2 teaspoons lime juice
1/2 cup heavy cream, whipped
1/2 cup shredded coconut

2 papayas
2 cups pineappple chunks
2 bananas, sliced
1/2 cup peanuts

Combine dressing and lime juice; mix well. Fold in whipped cream and 1/4 cup coconut. Chill. Cut papaya in half lengthwise; remove seeds. Remove papaya, leaving shells intact. Chop papaya; combine with remaining coconut, pineapple, banana and nuts; mix lightly. Spoon mixture into papaya shells; top with dressing.

4 servings

This salad is named for the ancient African civilization, Mali, where many of these popular fruits and nuts were common ingredients.

Tientsin Vegetable Platter

2 cups broccoli flowerets	2 cups cooked rice
2 cups celery slices	1/3 cup cashews, toasted
2 cups bean sprouts	1/4 cup green onion slices
1/2 lb. Chinese pea pods	1 qt. shredded lettuce
1 8-oz. bottle Kraft Italian dressing	

Place broccoli, celery, bean sprouts and pea pods in separate containers; pour 1/4 cup dressing over each vegetable. Cover; marinate in refrigerator overnight. Drain, reserving marinade. Combine 1/4 cup marinade, rice, nuts and onion; mix lightly. Arrange vegetables and rice on lettuce-covered platter. Serve with additional marinade, if desired.

8 to 10 servings

Variations: Substitute 6-oz. pkg. frozen pea pods for fresh.
Substitute 16-oz. can bean sprouts for fresh.

When purchasing fresh bean sprouts buy only the crispest, whitest sprouts to insure freshness.

Salad Niçoise

1 8-oz. bottle Kraft Italian dressing	2 medium tomatoes, cut into wedges
2 cups cooked potato slices	1 2-oz. can rolled anchovy fillets
1 cup cut green beans, cooked, drained	1/4 cup pitted ripe olives, cut in half
2 qts. torn assorted greens	1/4 cup green onion slices
1 6-1/2-oz. can tuna, drained, flaked	2 hard-cooked eggs, sliced

Pour dressing over potatoes and beans. Cover; marinate in refrigerator several hours. Drain, reserving marinade. Combine potatoes, beans, greens, tuna, tomato, anchovies, olives and onion; toss lightly. Garnish with eggs; serve with marinade.

6 servings

Tientsin Vegetable Platter, Salad Niçoise, Mali Fruit Salad (page 109)

Chow Mein Salad

2 cups chopped cooked pork,
    beef or chicken
1 1/2 cups cooked rice
1 16-oz. can bean sprouts,
    drained
1 cup celery slices
1 cup shredded carrot

1/2 cup green onion slices
1/4 cup chopped green
    pepper
Kraft French dressing
Salt and pepper
Lettuce

Combine meat, rice, vegetables and enough dressing to moisten; toss lightly. Season to taste. Chill. Serve in lettuce-lined bowl.

4 to 6 servings

Dublin Salad

1 8-oz. bottle Kraft coleslaw
    dressing
2 tablespoons Kraft pure
    prepared mustard
1/8 teaspoon caraway seed
2 cups cooked potato slices,
    chilled

1/2 lb. corned beef
4 ozs. Kraft natural
    Swiss cheese, cut
    into strips
1 qt. shredded cabbage

Combine dressing, mustard and caraway seed. Combine 1/4 cup dressing and potatoes; mix lightly. Arrange potatoes, meat and cheese on cabbage-covered platter. Serve with remaining dressing.

4 to 6 servings

Mediterranean Tuna Salad

3/4 cup Golden caesar dressing
1/2 cup dairy sour cream
2 6-1/2-oz. cans tuna,
    drained, flaked
1/2 cup pitted ripe olives,
    cut in half
1/2 cup celery slices

1/2 cup chopped green
    pepper
2 tablespoons chopped
    onion
1/8 teaspoon cracked black
    pepper
Romaine

Combine 1/2 cup dressing and sour cream; mix well. Chill. Combine remaining dressing, tuna, olives, celery, green pepper, onion and pepper; toss lightly. Serve on romaine. Top with dressing.

4 servings

SALADS

PICNICS, PARTIES, PORTABLES

Parties and picnics are convivial gatherings and the salads selected for such events should be equally festive. Depending on the occasion, salads can be casual or formal. Select a simple tossed salad, several relishes, potato salad or coleslaw for informal gatherings. For more elegant events, consider attractively layered or arranged salads or a fancy molded salad.

Partial or total do-ahead preparation is a great asset when entertaining and makes salads an ideal choice whatever the occasion. For picnic salads that travel, advanced planning is a "must." Portable salads should be thoroughly chilled and kept cold until eaten. Fortunately there is a wide variety of special vacuum containers or coolers available that will keep salads safely and refreshingly chilled for several hours. The ingredients for tossed and arranged salads can be prepared in advance and refrigerated in separate containers until just before serving.

Confetti Melon Bowl

1 8-oz. bottle Catalina
  French dressing
2 tablespoons honey
1 cup heavy cream, whipped
  Watermelon

Cantaloupe balls
Strawberries
Blueberries
Kraft miniature
  marshmallows

Combine dressing and honey; mix well. Fold in whipped cream. Chill. Cut off top third of watermelon. Scoop out melon balls, leaving shell intact. Cut zigzag pattern 1 inch deep around top of shell. Combine fruit and marshmallows in melon shell; mix lightly. Serve with dressing.

Layered Sea Salad (page 116), Confetti Melon Bowl, Super Salad Bar (page 116)

Layered Sea Salad

1 8-oz. bottle Kraft green
    goddess dressing
1/2 cup dairy sour cream
1 7-oz. pkg. shell macaroni,
    cooked, drained
1/4 cup chopped parsley

3 cups shredded lettuce
3 cups chopped tomatoes
1 1/2 cups celery slices
2 cups chopped cucumber
2 cups cleaned cooked
    shrimp

Combine dressing and sour cream; mix well. Chill. Combine macaroni and parsley; mix lightly. In 3 1/2-quart bowl, layer lettuce, tomato, celery, macaroni mixture, cucumber and shrimp. Chill. Serve with dressing.

8 to 10 servings

Variation: Substitute 16-oz. can salmon for shrimp.

For a decorative touch, garnish with celery leaves, cucumber twists or additional shrimp.

Super Salad Bar

1/2 cup Kraft Italian dressing
1/2 cup broccoli flowerets
1/2 cup mushroom slices
    *   *   *
1 1/2 qts. torn assorted greens
1/2 cup red onion rings
1/2 cup croutons
6 Boston lettuce cups
1 cup ham cubes

1 cup carrot curls
1 cup cherry tomato halves
6 ozs. Kraft sharp
    natural cheddar cheese,
    cut into strips
2 hard-cooked eggs,
    chopped
Assorted Kraft
    dressings

Pour Italian dressing over combined broccoli and mushrooms. Cover; marinate in refrigerator several hours. Drain.

Combine greens, onion and croutons in salad bowl; toss lightly. Place salad bowl in center of large platter; arrange lettuce cups around bowl. Fill lettuce cups with marinated vegetables, ham, carrot, tomato, cheese and eggs. Serve with dressings.

8 to 10 servings

Toss 'N Tote Coleslaw

1 qt. shredded cabbage
1/2 cup chopped green pepper
1/2 cup shredded carrot

1/4 cup chopped onion
1/3 cup Kraft coleslaw
    dressing

Combine ingredients; mix lightly. Chill. Add additional dressing before serving, if desired.

6 servings

Sierra Slaw

3 qts. shredded cabbage
2 cups shredded carrots
2 cups radish slices

1 cup green onion slices
1 16-oz. bottle Kraft
    French dressing

Combine ingredients; mix lightly. Chill overnight.

24 servings

Sweet 'N Sour Slaw

1 8-oz. bottle Kraft oil and
    vinegar dressing
1 cup cauliflowerets
1 11-oz. can mandarin orange
    segments, drained

1 8-1/4-oz. can pineapple
    chunks, drained
1/3 cup chopped green pepper
1 qt. shredded cabbage

Pour dressing over combined cauliflower, orange segments, pineapple and green pepper. Cover; marinate in refrigerator several hours. Drain, reserving 1/3 cup marinade. Combine marinade, vegetables, fruit and cabbage; toss lightly.

4 to 6 servings

Creamy Celery Salad

6 cups celery slices
2 cups pitted ripe olives
1 cup radish slices

1 teaspoon dill weed
3/4 cup Kraft creamy
    cucumber dressing

Combine ingredients; mix well. Chill.

8 to 10 servings

Take 'N Toss Salad

Torn assorted greens
Cherry tomatoes
Cucumber slices

Golden caesar or Kraft
golden blend Italian
dressing

Place greens and vegetables in plastic bag. Chill. Add dressing to salad just before serving; toss in plastic bag.

Jiffy Corn Relish

1 12-oz. can whole kernel
corn, drained
1/3 cup Catalina French dressing
1/3 cup chopped green pepper
1/4 cup chopped onion

2 tablespoons pickle
relish, drained
2 tablespoons chopped
pimiento
1/2 teaspoon celery seed

Combine ingredients; mix lightly. Chill overnight.

6 servings

Variation: Substitute 12-oz. can mexicorn for whole kernel corn.

Tasty Totin' Eggs

12 hard-cooked eggs
1/2 cup Kraft chunky blue
cheese dressing
1/2 cup finely chopped celery

2 tablespoons finely
chopped red pepper
4 crisply cooked bacon
slices, crumbled

Cut eggs in half. Remove yolks; mash. Blend in dressing, celery, red pepper and bacon; refill whites.

12 servings

Press egg halves together, wrap in plastic and tote to a picnic. What could be easier? But be sure to keep the eggs chilled.

Take 'N Toss Salad, Jiffy Corn Relish, Tasty Totin' Eggs

Portable Containers

When "toting" a salad to a party or picnic, consider these indispensables:

- Insulated coolers
- Wide-mouthed vacuum containers
- Moisture-vaporproof wrap
- Plastic bags
- Picnic baskets and tote bags
- Insulated bowls with tight-fitting covers

Cookout Macaroni Salad

1 7-1/4-oz. pkg. Kraft macaroni
    and cheese dinner
1/2 cup Miracle Whip salad
    dressing
1/2 cup Kraft French dressing

1/2 cup chopped pickle
1/4 cup chopped onion
8 crisply cooked bacon
    slices, crumbled
1 tomato, chopped

Prepare dinner as directed on package. Combine salad dressing and French dressing. Add to prepared dinner with remaining ingredients; mix lightly. Chill. Add additional French dressing before serving, if desired.

4 to 6 servings

Variation: This recipe can easily be doubled for a crowd.

Marinated Cucumbers

1 8-oz. bottle Kraft creamy
    Italian dressing
2 medium cucumbers, thinly
    sliced

2 small onions, thinly
    sliced

Combine ingredients; mix lightly. Chill several hours.

6 to 8 servings

A great "do-ahead" and a perfect choice for summer dining when fresh cucumbers are so readily available.

Buffet Tomato Platter

1 8-oz. bottle Kraft Italian
    dressing
4 cups cherry tomato halves

2 cups cucumber slices
1 1/2 cups chopped parsley
    Lettuce

Pour dressing over vegetables. Cover; marinate in refrigerator several hours. Drain, reserving marinade. Serve on lettuce-covered platter with marinade.

12 servings

Tossed Antipasto Salad

1 8-oz. bottle Kraft Italian
    or Golden caesar dressing
1 cup mushroom slices
1 cup cherry tomato halves
1 7-oz. can artichoke hearts,
    drained, halved

1 qt. torn spinach
2 cups torn assorted
    greens
1/2 cup croutons
    Kraft chunky blue
    cheese dressing

Pour Italian dressing over mushrooms, tomato and artichokes. Cover; marinate in refrigerator several hours or overnight. Drain, reserving 1/4 cup marinade. Combine marinade, vegetables and greens; toss lightly. Serve with croutons and blue cheese dressing.

6 servings

Gala Tossed Salad

1 garlic clove, peeled, cut
    in half
2 qts. torn assorted greens
1 11-oz. can mandarin orange
    segments, drained
1 cup green pepper strips

1 cup chopped cucumber
1 tomato, cut into wedges
    Kraft thousand island
    or creamy Russian
    dressing

Rub salad bowl with garlic. Combine greens, orange segments, green pepper, cucumber and tomato; toss lightly. Serve with dressing.

8 to 10 servings

Calico Salad Squares

2 3-oz. pkgs. lemon flavored gelatin	3/4 cup chopped tomato
1 teaspoon salt	1/3 cup chopped green onions
2 cups boiling water	1/4 cup chopped green pepper
1 1/2 cups cold water	Lettuce
2 tablespoons vinegar	Zesty Lemon Dressing
1 1/2 cups shredded carrot	

Dissolve gelatin and salt in boiling water. Add cold water and vinegar. Chill until partially set; fold in vegetables. Pour into 11 3/4 x 7 1/2-inch baking dish; chill until firm. Cut into squares; serve on lettuce-covered plate with:

Zesty Lemon Dressing

1/2 cup Kraft creamy Italian dressing	1/2 teaspoon grated lemon rind
1/2 cup Kraft real mayonnaise	

Combine dressing, mayonnaise and lemon rind; mix well. Chill.

8 to 10 servings

Rainbow Salad

2 qts. torn assorted greens	1/2 cup shredded coconut
1 cup strawberry halves	Catalina French dressing
2 bananas, sliced	

Combine greens, strawberries, bananas and coconut; toss lightly. Serve with dressing.

6 to 8 servings

Lemon Light Salad

1 8-oz. bottle Kraft oil and vinegar dressing	2 cups tomato slices
2 tablespoons lemon juice	1 cup cucumber slices
1 tablespoon chopped parsley	Romaine
1 teaspoon grated lemon rind	

Combine dressing, lemon juice, parsley and lemon rind; mix well. Arrange tomato and cucumber on individual lettuce-covered salad plates. Serve with dressing.

4 to 6 servings

Cranberry Orange Salad

1 1/2 cups cottage cheese
  1/2 teaspoon grated orange rind
  1 20-oz. can pineapple slices,
    drained
  1 16-oz. can jellied cranberry
    sauce, sliced

2 cups orange segments
Curly endive
Kraft Russian dressing

Combine cottage cheese and orange rind; chill. Place cottage cheese mixture on platter; surround with pineapple, cranberry sauce and oranges. Garnish with endive; serve with dressing.

6 servings

Citrus Fruit Basket

1 8-oz. bottle Catalina French
    dressing
1/3 cup dairy sour cream

6 large oranges
2 bananas, sliced
1 cup red grapes

Combine dressing and sour cream; mix well. Chill. Cut off top of oranges. Remove sections and membranes, leaving shell intact. Cut sections into chunks. Combine with bananas and grapes; mix lightly. Spoon fruit mixture into orange shells; serve with dressing.

6 servings

Paradise Papaya Boats

2 papayas
1 banana, sliced
1 cup strawberry halves
1/2 cup grape halves
1/4 cup macadamia nuts or
  almonds, toasted
1 tablespoon lime juice

* * *
1/2 cup Catalina French
  dressing
2 tablespoons honey
1 tablespoon lime juice
1/4 teaspoon grated
  lime rind

Cut papaya in half lengthwise. Remove seeds, reserving 1 tablespoon. Remove papaya, leaving shells intact. Cut papaya into chunks. Combine with bananas, strawberries, grapes, nuts and lime juice; mix lightly. Spoon mixture into papaya shells.

Place reserved papaya seeds and remaining ingredients in blender container; blend until smooth. Serve with fruit.

4 servings

Sherried Spinach Salad

1 8-oz. bottle Kraft oil and
    vinegar dressing
2 tablespoons sherry
1 qt. torn spinach
1 qt. torn assorted greens
1 cup mushroom slices

1/2 cup green onion slices
6 crisply cooked bacon
    slices, crumbled
2 hard-cooked egg yolks,
    sieved

Heat dressing and sherry in saucepan. Combine greens, mushrooms, onion and bacon. Add hot dressing; toss lightly. Top with eggs.

8 servings

Fruit 'N Greens Melon Basket

Watermelon
Honeydew melon balls
Torn assorted greens

Kiwi fruit slices
Toasted slivered almonds
Kraft Russian dressing

With sharp knife, make two vertical cuts 1 1/2 inches apart in center of watermelon one-third through fruit. From each end, cut watermelon horizontally to vertical cuts to form handle; remove sections. Scoop out fruit; cut into chunks. Cut zigzag pattern 1-inch deep around top of shell. Combine melon, greens and kiwi; toss lightly. Spoon into watermelon shell; sprinkle with nuts. Serve with dressing.

Summer Fruit Rainbow

1/2 cup Kraft French dressing
1 tablespoon honey
1/8 teaspoon coriander
1 cup whipped topping

2 cups peach slices
2 cups plum slices
2 cups nectarine slices
2 cups pear slices

Combine dressing, honey and coriander; mix well. Fold in whipped topping. Chill. In 2-quart glass bowl, layer peaches, plums, nectarines and pears; top with 1/2 cup dressing. Serve with remaining dressing.

8 to 10 servings

Make-Your-Own Salads

Torn assorted greens
Tomato wedges
Cucumber slices
Kraft grated parmesan cheese
Croutons
Crisply cooked bacon slices,
   crumbled
Canned kidney beans, drained

Stuffed green olive
   slices
Kraft Italian dressing
Kraft thousand island
   or creamy Russian
   dressing
Roka brand blue cheese
   dressing

Combine greens, tomato and cucumber; toss lightly. Arrange separate bowls of greens mixture, cheese, croutons, bacon, beans and olives. Serve with dressings as make-your-own salads.

Smorgasbords are the forerunners of contemporary salad bars, a popular serving style in restaurants and for home entertaining. Attractive, easy and efficient, buffet service is ideally suited to large gatherings and outdoor dining where guests can serve themselves.

Any type of salad from appetizer to dessert can be served buffet style. A create-your-own salad arrangement is particularly colorful and inviting. Guests can custom-design salads from an assortment of fruits, vegetables, meats, toppings and dressings, imaginatively assembled on a table, buffet or counter. A variety of salads served as a complete meal are especially welcome for potluck suppers, luncheons and late evening gatherings. Plan a menu including a variety of styles — tossed, layered, molded or arranged. Casual or formal salad bars are right in style with today's easy living.

Safety Tips

A few safety precautions are essential for salads that travel.

- The big three in the rule department are:
  - Keep foods clean.
  - Keep hot foods hot — 140°F or above.
  - Keep cold foods cold — 40°F or below.
- For cold foods, be sure the salad and container are thoroughly chilled and keep them that way until they reach their destination.
- Chill vacuum containers overnight or rinse with cold water.
- At the last minute, pack cold salads directly from refrigerator into a well-insulated chest filled with dry ice packs or ice cubes.
- Transport hot salads in well-insulated vacuum containers. If possible, reheat at the party or picnic.
- Place picnic baskets and chests inside the car, away from the sun's rays. Never carry food in the trunk where temperatures are much higher.
- Contrary to popular belief, mayonnaise and salad dressings cannot cause food poisoning because the acidity of these products does not allow the bacterial growth associated with food poisoning. However, when low-acid foods such as eggs, vegetables, meat, poultry and fish are combined with these dressings, the resulting mixture (a potato salad, for example) can become a source of food illness.

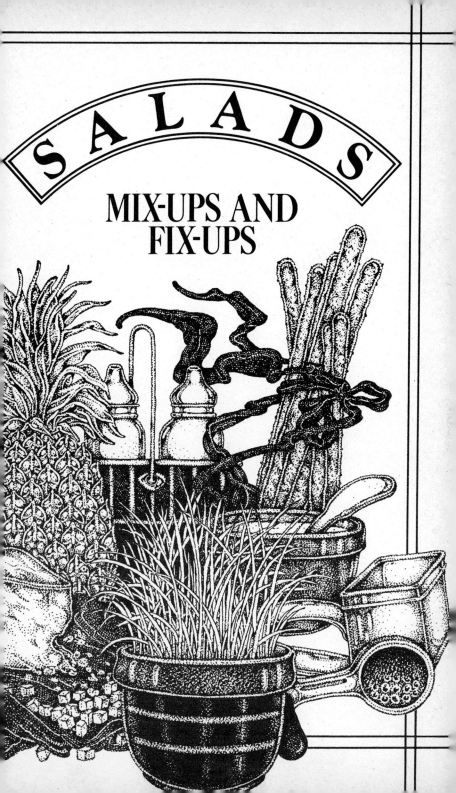

SALADS

MIX-UPS AND FIX-UPS

There is much more to creating an attractive, appetizing salad than just skillfully selecting and combining ingredients. Equally important to salad artistry is knowing how to "mix up" new dressings and to "fix up" salads with decorative garnishes or flavorful toppings. Many interesting dressings can be quickly and easily created by combining two prepared dressings or by adding one or two ingredients such as an herb, chopped parsley or grated parmesan cheese. Garnishes can be as simple as a sprig of watercress, a few celery leaves or a sprinkling of shredded carrots. Fancy garnishes require some extra time and skill, but are worth the effort for special occasions. Remember that excessive garnishing can be garish, detracting from the natural beauty of the salad. "Less is more" is a good guideline to follow.

Polynesian Dressing

1 8-oz. bottle Kraft thousand island or creamy Russian dressing
1/4 cup crushed pineapple, drained
2 tablespoons finely chopped green pepper
1/2 teaspoon celery seed

Combine ingredients; mix well. Chill. Serve over assorted greens or fruit.

1 1/4 cups

Appleicious French Dressing

3/4 cup Kraft French dressing
1/4 cup applesauce

Combine ingredients; mix well. Serve with fruit salads.

1 cup

Sweet 'N Sour French Dressing

1 8-oz. bottle Kraft oil and vinegar dressing

1/4 cup Kraft orange marmalade

Combine ingredients, mix well. Chill. Serve with lettuce.

1 1/4 cups

Creamy Fruit Dressing

1/2 cup Kraft Russian dressing

1 cup dairy sour cream

Combine ingredients, mix well. Serve with fruit salads.

1 1/2 cups

Zesty Dressing

1 8-oz. bottle Kraft thousand island or creamy Russian dressing

1/4 cup Horseradish

Combine ingredients; mix well. Serve with seafood salads.

1 cup

Sherry French Dressing

1/2 cup Catalina French dressing

2 tablespoons sherry

Combine ingredients; mix well. Serve with assorted greens.

1/2 cup

Glorious French Dressing

1 8-oz. bottle Kraft French dressing
2 tablespoons honey

1 teaspoon lemon juice
1 teaspoon grated lemon rind

Combine ingredients; mix well. Serve with fruit salads.

1 cup

Gourmet Dressing

1 8-oz. bottle Kraft thousand
island or creamy Russian
dressing
2 tablespoons Kraft chopped
blue cheese crumbles

2 crisply cooked bacon
slices, crumbled
1 tablespoon milk

Combine ingredients; mix well. Chill. Serve over lettuce.

1 1/4 cups

Fluffy French Dressing

1 8-oz. bottle Kraft French
dressing
1/4 cup honey
1/4 teaspoon ground coriander

1/2 cup heavy cream,
whipped

Combine dressing, honey and coriander; mix well. Fold in whipped cream. Serve with fruit.

Approximately 2 cups

Regal Cheese Dressing

1 8-oz. bottle Catalina French
dressing
1 4-oz. pkg. Kraft chopped
blue cheese crumbles

4 crisply cooked bacon
slices, crumbled

Combine ingredients; mix well. Chill. Serve with vegetable and main dish salads.

1 1/2 cups

Curry Dressing

1/2 cup Kraft Russian dressing   1/2 teaspoon curry powder

Combine ingredients; mix well. Chill. Serve with assorted greens or ham salad.

1/2 cup

Marvelous Mix-Ups

For instant innovation, blend two compatible dressings. Here are a few flavorful suggestions.

Blend . . .

1/2 cup Kraft or Catalina French dressing	and	1/4 cup Kraft Italian dressing
1/4 cup Kraft French or garlic French dressing	and	1 cup Kraft real mayonnaise
1/2 cup Catalina French dressing	and	1 cup Miracle Whip salad dressing
1 8-oz. bottle Kraft chunky or Roka brand blue cheese dressing	and	1/4 cup Kraft French or garlic French dressing
1/2 cup Kraft thousand island or creamy Russian dressing	and	1/4 cup Kraft chunky or Roka brand blue cheese dressing

El Paso Sauce

1/2 cup celery slices
1/2 cup chopped green pepper
1/4 cup chopped onion

3/4 cup Catalina French dressing
1 cup chopped tomato

Cook celery, green pepper and onion in small amount of dressing over low heat until tender. Add remaining dressing and tomato; heat. Serve over lettuce wedges or ground beef patties.

1 1/4 cups

Sauce Deluxe

1 8-oz. bottle Kraft coleslaw dressing
1 tablespoon Kraft pure prepared mustard

Dash of Worcestershire sauce

Combine ingredients; mix well. Chill. Serve over vegetables.

1 cup

Cocktail Sauce

1 8-oz. bottle Kraft thousand
  island or creamy Russian
  dressing
2 tablespoons green onion
  slices

2 tablespoons chopped
  green pepper
1/8 teaspoon hot pepper
  sauce

Combine ingredients; mix well. Chill. Add additional hot pepper sauce, if desired. Serve with seafood.

1 cup

Favorite Croutons

2 cups white bread cubes

1/4 cup Parkay margarine,
  melted

Toss bread cubes with margarine; place in ungreased baking pan. Bake at 400°, 5 to 10 minutes or until lightly browned, stirring occasionally.

1 cup

Variations: Substitute whole-wheat, rye or raisin bread.
          Substitute French bread and toss with
            2 tablespoons Kraft grated parmesan cheese.

Golden Crisp Croutons

2 cups Italian bread cubes
1/4 cup Kraft golden blend
  Italian dressing

Toss bread cubes with dressing; place on ungreased baking pan. Bake at 350°, 20 minutes, stirring occasionally.

1 1/2 cups

Crunchy Salad Topper

2 cups old fashioned or quick
   oats, uncooked
1/2 cup Kraft oil and vinegar
   dressing

1/3 cup Kraft grated
   parmesan cheese
1/3 cup wheat germ

Combine ingredients; mix well. Pour mixture onto ungreased 15 1/2 x 10 1/2-inch jelly roll pan. Bake at 350°, 15 to 18 minutes or until golden brown. Cool; refrigerate in tightly covered container. Sprinkle over salads.

3 cups

Easy Fix-Ups

Simple or fancy, garnishes can make a plain salad festive. A few fix-ups for inspiration . . .

- Shredded carrots or zucchini
- Sprigs of parsley, watercress or mint
- Red or white onion rings
- Curly endive
- Sliced, shredded or sieved hard-cooked eggs
- Tomato wedges or slices
- Celery leaves
- Orange or grapefruit sections
- Flaked or shredded coconut
- Black or green olive slices
- Shredded red cabbage

Crunchy Fix-Ups

Add a little crunch to your salads with these easy fix-ups:

- Crisply cooked bacon, crumbled
- French fried onion rings
- Crushed potato or corn chips
- Alfalfa or bean sprouts
- Chopped peanuts, walnuts or pecans
- Sliced or slivered almonds, toasted
- Apple or pear wedges
- Pomegranate seeds
- Shredded coconut, toasted
- Bite-size crispy rice or wheat squares
- Croutons
- Chow mein noodles
- Shoestring potatoes

Cheesy Fix-Ups

For a piquant touch, sprinkle your salads with . . .

- Shredded cheddar, Swiss or mozzarella cheese
- Grated parmesan or romano cheese
- Crumbled blue or Roquefort cheese
- Cheese cubes
- Cheese slices cut into julienne strips

Fancy Fix-Ups

For that extra special occasion, decorate your salad with . . .

- **Flowers** — Diagonally slice carrots, beets, cucumber or zucchini; arrange flower fashion with olives for centers and parsley or watercress sprigs for stems and leaves.
- **Tomato Flowers** — Cut tomato into wedges almost to stem end; spread slightly.
- **Pinwheels** — Cut tomatoes or hard-cooked eggs into wedges; arrange pinwheel fashion with celery leaves.
- **Carrot Curls** — Cut thin lengthwise strips of carrot with a vegetable peeler. Curl strips around your finger; secure with picks. Chill in ice water for at least an hour until curls are crisp. Remove picks.
- **Celery Fans** — Cut celery into 1-inch pieces; thinly slice one end. Chill in ice water until cut ends begin to curl.
- **Pickle Fans** — Thinly slice pickles almost to stem end; spread slices.
- **Radish Roses** — Trim off root; cut outer layer petal fashion from top almost to stem end. Chill in ice water until petals open.
- **Twists** — Make a cut in cucumber, lemon, lime or orange slice from edge to center. Twist and stand upright.
- **Frosted Fruit** — Rinse and dry grapes, cranberries or cherries. Dip in egg white, beaten until frothy, and then in granulated sugar. Shake off excess sugar; let dry.

SALADS

ETC. ETC. ETC.

Although dressings are generally accepted as the natural companions of salads, they are really quite versatile. Zesty dressings such as Italian, Russian and caesar are ideal marinades for meat, fish or kabobs. Almost any clear or creamy dressing adds flavor interest to hot cooked vegetables. Creamy dressings — cucumber, garlic, chunky blue cheese and thousand island — are attractive, piquant sauces for open-face sandwiches, beef patties and baked potatoes. Tomato based dressings are especially compatible with chicken and seafood dishes. Dressings also provide seasoning and a rich sauce for many casseroles, stews and chowders. Your own imagination is sure to suggest many other cooking possibilities.

Chicken Marseilles

1 2-1/2 to 3-lb. broiler-fryer,
   cut up
Catalina French dressing
1 16-oz. can tomatoes
8 onion slices, 1/4-inch thick
1 teaspoon salt
1/2 teaspoon celery seed
1/4 teaspoon pepper
1/4 cup wine or water
2 tablespoons flour

Brown chicken in 1/3 cup dressing over low heat. Add 1/4 cup dressing, tomatoes, onion and seasonings. Cover; simmer 45 minutes. Remove chicken and vegetables to serving platter. Gradually add wine to flour, stirring until well blended. Gradually add flour mixture to hot liquid in pan; cook, stirring constantly, until mixture boils and thickens. Simmer 3 minutes, stirring constantly. Serve with chicken and vegetables.

4 servings

Chicken Marseilles

Kabobs Italiano

1 8-oz. bottle Kraft golden
    blend Italian dressing
1 1/2 lbs. lamb or beef, cut into
    1-inch cubes
2 cups zucchini slices

2 cups mushrooms
1 8-oz. can small whole
    onions, drained
1 cup green pepper chunks

Pour dressing over meat and vegetables. Cover; marinate in refrigerator several hours or overnight. Drain, reserving marinade. Alternate meat and vegetables on skewers. Broil 15 to 20 minutes or to desired doneness, turning and brushing frequently with marinade. Serve over hot cooked rice, if desired.

4 to 6 servings

Countryside Ragout

2 lbs. beef or lamb, cut into
    1-inch cubes
1/4 cup flour
3/4 cup Kraft French dressing
3/4 cup water

12 small onions
1 cup carrot sticks
1 cup mushroom slices
2 cups hot mashed
    potatoes

Coat meat with flour; brown in 1/4 cup dressing over low heat. Add remaining dressing and water. Cover; simmer 1 hour. Add onion and carrot; continue simmering 30 minutes or until meat and vegetables are tender. Add mushrooms; pour into 2-quart casserole. Spoon potatoes around edge. Broil 5 minutes or until lightly browned.

6 servings

Shashlik

Kraft Russian dressing
1 lb. round steak, 1/4-inch
    thick, cut into strips
1 1/2 cups cherry tomatoes
1/4 lb. mushroom caps

1 16-oz. can whole
    potatoes, drained
1 zucchini, cut into
    chunks

Pour dressing over meat. Cover; marinate in refrigerator several hours or overnight. Drain, reserving marinade. Alternate meat and vegetables on skewers accordion style. Broil or grill 10 to 12 minutes, turning and brushing frequently with marinade.

6 servings

Man-Size Sandwiches

1 lb. thin roast beef slices
1 cup onion rings
3/4 cup Kraft Italian dressing
3/4 cup thin green pepper rings

4 to 6 hard rolls, split,
heated

Combine meat, onion and dressing in skillet. Cook over low heat 15 minutes, stirring occasionally. Add green pepper; continue cooking 5 minutes. For each sandwich, cover bottom half of roll with meat mixture. Cover with top half of roll.

4 to 6 sandwiches

Saucy Veal Schnitzel

1 1/2 lbs. veal steak
1/2 cup Kraft French dressing
1 1/2 cups water
1 cup onion rings
1/2 teaspoon caraway seed

2 tablespoons flour
1 cup dairy sour cream
4 cups (8 ozs.) noodles,
cooked, drained

Cut meat into 1/4-inch strips. Brown meat in 1/4 cup dressing over low heat. Add remaining dressing, 1 cup water, onion and caraway seed. Cover; simmer 20 minutes or until meat is tender. Remove meat and vegetables to serving platter. Gradually add remaining water to flour, stirring until well blended. Gradually add flour mixture to hot liquid in pan; cook, stirring constantly, until mixture boils and thickens. Stir in sour cream. Serve with meat and vegetables over noodles.

4 to 6 servings

Green Onion Omelet

1 tablespoon green onion slices
2 tablespoons Parkay margarine
4 eggs, slightly beaten

1/3 cup Kraft green onion
dressing
1/3 cup chopped ham

Sauté onion in margarine. Combine eggs, dressing and ham; pour into skillet. Cook slowly. As egg mixture sets, lift slightly with spatula to allow uncooked portion to flow underneath. Slip turner underneath, tip skillet to loosen and gently fold in half.

2 servings

141

Zesty Hero

1/2 cup Kraft golden blend
    Italian dressing
1 cup chopped tomato
1/2 cup onion rings
1/4 cup chopped green pepper

1 French bread loaf
Lettuce
Assorted luncheon
    meat slices

Pour dressing over combined tomato, onion and green pepper. Cover; marinate in refrigerator several hours. Drain, reserving marinade. Cut bread lengthwise to within 1/2 inch of bottom crust. Brush cut surface of bread with marinade; fill with lettuce, meat and marinated vegetables. Slice to serve.

4 to 6 servings

Town House Chicken Sandwich

2 cups chopped cooked chicken
1 avocado, peeled, chopped
1 cup cherry tomato halves
1/4 teaspoon salt
    Dash of pepper
1 8-oz. bottle Kraft thousand
    island or creamy Russian
    dressing

4 rye bread slices
4 lettuce cups
1 hard-cooked egg,
    chopped

Combine chicken, avocado, tomato, salt and pepper; mix lightly. For each sandwich, spread one bread slice with dressing; top with lettuce and chicken mixture. Garnish with egg; serve with remaining dressing.

4 sandwiches

Zucchini Italienne

4 cups zucchini slices
1/2 cup pitted ripe olives

1/4 cup Golden caesar
    dressing

Combine ingredients in 10-inch skillet. Cover; simmer over low heat 20 minutes or until zucchini is tender, stirring occasionally.

6 servings

Zesty Hero, Town House Chicken Sandwich

Oriental Pork

1 1/2 lbs. pork, cut into strips
1 8-oz. bottle Catalina
   French dressing
1 cup water
1 teaspoon ginger
1/4 teaspoon salt
1/4 teaspoon cayenne

3 tablespoons cornstarch
2 tablespoons soy sauce
2 cups shredded bok choy
   leaves or lettuce
1/2 cup green onion slices
1/2 cup celery slices
Hot cooked rice

Brown pork in 1/4 cup dressing over low heat. Add remaining dressing, water and seasonings. Cover; simmer 30 minutes. Gradually add combined cornstarch and soy sauce; simmer until mixture is thickened. Stir in bok choy, onion and celery; heat thoroughly, stirring occasionally. Serve over rice.

6 servings

Red Rice

1/2 lb. cooked smoked sausage,
   cut into slices
1 3/4 cups water
1 16-oz. can tomatoes
1 cup rice
1/2 cup Catalina French dressing

1/2 cup chopped green pepper
1/2 cup chopped onion
1 teaspoon salt
1/4 teaspoon hot pepper
   sauce
Dash of pepper

Combine ingredients; bring to boil. Cover; simmer 30 to 35 minutes or until rice is tender, stirring occasionally.

6 to 8 servings

Poulet Français

1 2-1/2 to 3-lb. broiler-fryer,
   cut up
1/4 cup flour
   Dash of salt and pepper

3/4 cup Roka brand blue
   cheese dressing

Coat chicken with combined flour and seasonings; dip in dressing. Place in 11 3/4 x 7 1/2-inch baking dish. Bake at 350°, 50 to 60 minutes or until tender.

4 servings

Jiffy Spaghetti Sauce

1 lb. ground beef
1/2 cup chopped onion
1 16-oz. can tomatoes, drained
1 8-oz. can tomato sauce

1/2 cup Kraft red wine
    vinegar and oil
    dressing
2 tablespoons flour

Brown meat; drain. Add onion; cook until tender. Stir in tomatoes and tomato sauce. Gradually add dressing to flour, stirring until well blended; stir into sauce. Cover; simmer 15 minutes. Serve over hot cooked spaghetti.

4 servings

A short-cut spaghetti sauce seasoned with spicy dressing! Garlic bread and a crisp tossed salad are nice accompaniments for a spaghetti dinner.

Gourmet Hamburgers

1 1/2 lbs. ground beef
1/2 cup chopped onion
    Kraft chunky blue cheese
      dressing

Hamburger buns, split,
    toasted
Lettuce

Combine meat, onion and 1/4 cup dressing; mix lightly. Shape into six patties. Grill or broil on both sides to desired doneness. For each sandwich, cover bottom half of bun with lettuce, beef patty and dressing. Cover with top half of bun.

6 servings

Monterey Sandwich

4 whole-wheat bread slices
1 8-oz. bottle Kraft thousand
    island or creamy Russian
    dressing
1/2 cup alfalfa sprouts
1 6-oz. pkg. Kraft natural
    monterey jack cheese slices

1 cup avocado rings
12 ozs. cooked sliced
    turkey
8 crisply cooked bacon
    slices

For each sandwich, spread bread slice with dressing. Cover with alfalfa sprouts, cheese, avocado, turkey and bacon. Serve with additional dressing.

4 sandwiches

Pasta Primavera

2 cups broccoli flowerets
2 cups mushroom slices
2 cups 1-inch zucchini sticks
1 1/2 cups 1-inch asparagus pieces
3/4 cup Kraft Italian dressing
1 cup Kraft creamy garlic
  dressing
1/2 cup (2 ozs.) Kraft grated
  parmesan cheese

1/3 cup half and half
12 ozs. spaghetti, cooked,
  drained
2 cups chopped tomato
2 tablespoons chopped
  parsley
1/4 cup pine nuts, toasted

Sauté broccoli, mushrooms, zucchini and asparagus in 1/4 cup Italian dressing. Combine garlic dressing, cheese and half and half. Add spaghetti; toss lightly. Add sautéed vegetables; mix lightly over low heat until thoroughly heated. Sauté tomato and parsley in remaining Italian dressing. Serve over spaghetti; sprinkle with nuts.

8 servings

Shrimp Creole

1 16-oz. can tomatoes
1 8-oz. bottle Catalina French
  dressing
1/2 cup chopped onion
1/2 cup chopped green pepper

2 tablespoons water
1 tablespoon flour
1 lb. cleaned cooked
  shrimp
Hot cooked rice

Combine tomatoes, dressing, onion and green pepper. Cover; simmer 20 minutes. Gradually add water to flour, stirring until well blended. Gradually add flour mixture to hot liquid in pan; cook, stirring constantly, until mixture boils and thickens. Simmer 3 minutes, stirring constantly. Add shrimp; heat. Serve over rice.

4 servings

A quick and easy version of a famous New Orleans favorite. The spicy dressing adds extra flavor.

Prairieland Pot Roast

1 3 to 4-lb. pot roast
Salt and pepper
1 8-oz. bottle Catalina
  French dressing
1/2 cup water
8 small onions

4 medium carrots, cut
  into 1-inch pieces
4 potatoes, peeled,
  quartered
1/2 cup water
1/4 cup flour

Season meat with salt and pepper. Brown in 1/4 cup dressing over low heat. Add remaining dressing and water. Cover; simmer 2 hours. Add onion, carrot and potatoes. Cover; continue simmering 1 hour or until meat and vegetables are tender. Remove meat and vegetables to serving platter. Gradually add water to flour, stirring until well blended. Gradually add flour mixture to hot liquid in pan; cook, stirring constantly, until mixture boils and thickens. Simmer about 5 minutes, stirring constantly. Serve with meat and vegetables.

6 to 8 servings

Braised German Cabbage

1 1/2 qts. shredded red cabbage
1 cup chopped onion
1/2 cup Catalina French dressing

1/3 cup water
1/2 teaspoon caraway seed
1/4 teaspoon salt

Combine cabbage, onion, dressing, water and seasonings in large skillet. Cover; cook over low heat 20 to 25 minutes or until cabbage is tender, stirring occasionally.

6 servings

Pepper Relish

2 cups finely chopped green
  pepper
2 cups finely chopped red
  pepper
1 1/2 cups finely chopped onion

1/2 cup Kraft French or
  Catalina French
  dressing

Combine vegetables and dressing in saucepan. Cover; cook over low heat 15 minutes, stirring occasionally. Chill overnight.

8 to 10 servings

Reuben Sandwiches

12 rye bread slices
1 8-oz. bottle Kraft thousand
  island or creamy Russian
  dressing
1 lb. corned beef slices

1 8-oz. pkg. Kraft natural
  Swiss cheese slices
1 8-oz. can sauerkraut,
  rinsed, drained
Parkay margarine

For each sandwich, spread two bread slices with dressing; fill with meat, cheese and sauerkraut. Spread outside of sandwich with margarine; grill until lightly browned on both sides. Serve with additional dressing, if desired.

6 sandwiches

Regency Ratatouille

2 cups zucchini slices
1/2 cup green pepper strips
1/2 cup Catalina French dressing

2 cups mushroom slices
1 1/2 cups cherry tomato
  halves

Combine zucchini, green pepper and dressing in skillet. Simmer over low heat 10 minutes, stirring occasionally. Add mushrooms and tomato; continue cooking until mushrooms are tender.

6 to 8 servings

SALADS
ALL GOOD THINGS

Nutritious, delicious, attractive and versatile are just a few of the many "good things" about salads. Best of all, almost any food, in any form — fresh, frozen, canned or packaged — is suitable for salads. A stroll through your neighborhood grocery or supermarket will quickly verify this claim. Every department has something to offer, ranging from fresh produce to packaged pasta. Also, notice the many convenient dressings — creamy, chunky, savory, sweet, tart — ready to serve with the salad of your choice.

Ingredient variety is perhaps the greatest salad asset. Because it is easy to vary the ingredients, salads are very versatile and can be adapted to any meal, occasion or position in the menu. They can be served for brunch, lunch or dinner as appetizers, accompaniments, main dishes or desserts. It simply depends on the selection of ingredients and the size of the serving. Salads also can be made in many styles: casually tossed or mixed, attractively arranged or layered, imaginatively molded or even heated. With a little artistry and planning, salads can highlight the menu by adding variety and contrasts in color, flavors, textures and shapes.

A Few Considerations

In selecting a recipe or designing your own salad, advanced planning can spare last minute preparation and help assure success. Before making a salad, here are a few thoughts to ponder.

Meal Situation: For what meal is the salad intended and what is the occasion — family meal, picnic, celebration, party or potluck?

Menu Balance: Salad ingredients should complement, not duplicate, other foods in the menu. For example, serve simple salads with hearty casseroles, well-seasoned salads with mild foods and crunchy salads with creamy main dishes.

Position in the Menu: Salad size depends on when it is to be served. Allow about 1/2 cup per serving for appetizer salads; 1/2 to 1 cup for accompaniment salads; 1 to 3 cups for main dishes; and 1/2 to 3/4 cup for dessert salads. The larger portions are for salads made with greens.

Nutritive Value: Variety is one of the best ways to provide good nutritive value. The basic food groups are a good guide to follow.

Appetite Appeal: Salads should please the eye as well as the palate. Their ingredients can offer contrasts in colors, flavors, textures and shapes. For example — combine light and bright colors, strong and mild flavors, crunchy and smooth textures, chopped and sliced ingredients.

Preparation Time: Keep the salad simple on busy days — a few lettuce leaves, zucchini slices, tomato wedges and a flavorful creamy dressing. When life is more leisurely, mold a salad, arrange a colorful platter of fruits and vegetables for a salad buffet or seek an exotic ingredient or two — bok choy, kiwi fruit, mangoes, pomegranates.

Good-For-You Foods

A quick and easy guide for selecting salad ingredients is the basic food groups which provide the nutrients needed by the body for:

- Growth and repair of tissue
- Energy and heat
- Regulating bodily functions

Dairy Products provide calcium, protein, riboflavin (vitamin B_2), phosphorus and vitamin D.
The major food sources are milk, cottage cheese, natural and process cheese, sour cream, yogurt and ice cream.

Meat and Alternatives provide protein, niacin, iron, thiamine (vitamin B_1) and phosphorus.
The major food sources are lean meat, poultry,

seafood, eggs, natural and process cheese, dried peas and beans, nuts and peanut butter.

Fruits and Vegetables provide vitamins A and C, carbohydrates, minerals, water and fiber.

The major food sources for vitamin A are apricots, broccoli, cantaloupe, carrots, chard, collards, cress, persimmons, pumpkin, spinach, kale, mangoes, mustard and turnip greens and papaya.

The major food sources of vitamin C are broccoli, Brussels sprouts, cantaloupe, grapefruit, green pepper, oranges, strawberries, sweet red pepper, asparagus, blackberries, cabbage, cauliflower, chard, collards, endive, kale, melons, mustard greens, potatoes, raspberries and tomatoes.

Breads and Cereals provide carbohydrates, thiamine (vitamin B_1), niacin, riboflavin (vitamin B_2) and iron.

The major food sources are macaroni; noodles; rice; and whole grain, fortified or enriched breads and cereals.

When planning a salad or selecting recipes, be sure that at least one or two foods from the basic groups are included. Then add as many other compatible foods as desired. All foods contain nutrients but to a lesser degree than these key sources. Choosing foods from the basic food groups not only guarantees good nutritive value but automatically assures a variety of colors, flavors, textures and shapes — the attributes of a beautiful and delicious salad.

SALAD SAVVY

For the novice chef or the aspiring epicure, learning the language and conquering a few basic techniques is the quickest route to salad-making success. Scan the following list for terms that may have confused or eluded you in the past.

Accompaniment Salad — A fruit or vegetable salad served with, or just before or after, the main course.

Appetizer Salad — A small salad which whets the appetite and lends zest and flavor to the meal. Served with or without lettuce, it appears before the meal or as a first course.

Blend — Thoroughly combine two or more ingredients or prepare food in an electric blender or mixer.

Chill — Refrigerate until cold.

Chop — Cut into pieces of random size.

Coat — Cover surface of food evenly.

Combine — Put ingredients together and mix well until uniformly distributed.

Cool — Allow to come to room temperature.

Croutons — Small cubes of bread usually tossed with melted margarine or oil, then oven-toasted or sautéed until crisp. Croutons are used as garnishes for salads and soups and may be seasoned with pourable dressings.

Crudités — Raw vegetables or fruits served as appetizers, often with a dip.

Cube — Cut into pieces of uniform size and shape, usually 1/2 inch or larger.

Cut into Wedges — Cut vegetables, fruit or meat into triangular shapes.

Dash — Add less than 1/8 teaspoon of an ingredient.

Dessert Salad — A sweet salad, often molded or frozen, served at the end of a meal.

Drain — Separate liquid from solids by placing food in a colander or strainer.

Firm — In regard to molded gelatin salads, the gelatin mixture in the mold does not move when tilted and does not stick to the fingers. At this point, the salad is "set" and ready for unmolding.

Flake — Gently separate cooked seafood into very small pieces.

Fold In — Combine delicate ingredients such as beaten egg whites or whipped cream with other ingredients. Gently cut down the center of the mixture, across the bottom of the bowl and up and over the top of the mixture, using a circular motion.

Garnish — Edible decoration added to a finished dish that enhances the appearance.

Heavy Cream — Cream that has a fat content of at least 36% and is generally used for whipping. Heavy cream is also referred to as whipping cream.

Julienne — Cut food into thin slivers or strips. Ham, turkey, vegetables and cheeses are often cut into julienne strips for salads.

Main Dish Salad — A hearty salad which contains protein foods and is the major dish in the meal. It is often a complete meal.

Marinade — Any liquid, usually an oil-acid mixture such as French dressing, in which food is marinated for the purpose of absorbing flavor from the liquid.

Marinate — Let food stand in a seasoned liquid, such as dressings, for a period of time to produce flavor. Use glass, ceramic, plastic or stainless steel containers for marinating because the acid in the dressings can pit unglazed pottery, aluminum, cast iron and copper.

Partially Set — Stage of thickening for gelatin mixture when it is the consistency of unbeaten egg whites. At this stage fold in other ingredients.

Peel — Remove skin or a thin outer layer from a fruit or vegetable.

Pourable Dressing — A dressing that can be poured.

Sauté — Brown or cook in a small amount of hot fat.

Section — To remove a portion of fruit by separating connective membrane with a knife. This is in regard to fruits such as grapefruit and oranges which are comprised of separate but connected portions.
Shred — Cut into very thin pieces using a shredder or knife.
Tear — Break into bite-size pieces.
Toss — Mix lightly with a lifting motion, using two forks or spoons.
Whip — Beat rapidly with a wire whisk, rotary beater or electric mixer to incorporate air and increase volume.

EQUIPPED FOR ACTION

One of the great attractions of salads is the ease of preparation. Much of the ease, however, depends on the right equipment. With some basic tools and a few specialty items, you are all set for action.

The Basics

Cutting Board — Select a hardwood or durable plastic board that can withstand repeated slicing and chopping.
French Knife — Several versions are available, but all have long broad blades that taper to a sharp point.
Paring or Utility Knife — Both are used for slicing or chopping small ingredients and are especially effective for paring produce or preparing intricate garnishes.
Serrated Knife — Several types are available, but all have saw-toothed blades. Excellent for slicing tender ingredients such as tomatoes.
Strainer or Colander — A large strainer or colander is useful for draining greens and canned fruit or vegetables; a small, fine strainer for straining juices, relishes, capers, shredded cucumber and similar items.

Kitchen Shears — Shears or rust-proof scissors are ideal for snipping chives, parsley or green onion stems.

Shredder — Several sizes are advantageous for shredding or grating such diverse ingredients as onion, carrot, cucumber, zucchini, cheese and hard-cooked eggs.

Peeler — The stainless steel variety is best because it will not discolor fruits and vegetables.

Specialties

Egg and Tomato Slicers — These tools are important time-savers because they cut several uniform slices at one time.

Melon Ball Cutter — Most versions have a large and small cutter at opposite ends of a slim handle — ideal for scooping attractive, uniform balls from melons and avocados.

French Salad Basket — A flexible wire basket for draining and fluffing greens.

Corer — A small cylindrical tool with a sharp point for coring apples and pears.

Chopping Bowl and Chopper — These are especially quick and safe for chopping small ingredients such as parsley, chives, nuts, green pepper and onion.

INDEX